旅游职业英语

Professional Tourism English

刘红梅　李丽萍　李雨桐　主编

化学工业出版社

·北京·

内容简介

《旅游职业英语》是以游客的"旅游过程"为主线，串联旅行社、酒店、航空公司相关工作岗位的工作内容和工作流程，以真人拍摄的实际案例模拟旅游行程安排和旅游过程管理。分为总体介绍、出团前工作、导引服务、酒店安排、机场服务、客户关系维护六大模块，共20个单元。主要内容包括：旅游过程中相关岗位的具体工作内容和流程；著名国际酒店集团概况以及旅游行业发展趋势；签证办理相关知识；四川著名景点的英文讲解；旅游活动六大要素"吃、住、行、游、购、娱"的常用英语词汇和旅游行业的英语专有名词；旅行社、机场、酒店、景点游览、餐厅、娱乐场所、免税店等不同情境下旅游接待的常用英语交际表达方式；酒店预订单、客房登记单、洗衣单、通告、菜单、旅游计划安排等旅游文案的写作等。

书中配有65个同步真人视频和音频，以帮助读者有效提升英语对客服务能力。本书主要供旅游管理专业群（含导游、酒店管理、空乘）两年或三年制职业院校师生教学使用，也可供想学习旅游英语和从事旅游行业相关工作的社会人员参考。

图书在版编目（CIP）数据

旅游职业英语/刘红梅，李丽萍，李雨桐主编.—北京：化学工业出版社，2020.8（2024.8重印）

ISBN 978-7-122-37647-3

Ⅰ.①旅… Ⅱ.①刘… ②李… ③李… Ⅲ.①旅游-英语 Ⅳ.①F59

中国版本图书馆CIP数据核字（2020）第161755号

责任编辑：章梦婕　　　　　　　　　　　　　　　　装帧设计：王晓宇
责任校对：王　静

出版发行：化学工业出版社（北京市东城区青年湖南街13号　邮政编码100011）
印　　装：涿州市殷润文化传播有限公司
787mm×1092mm　1/16　印张11　字数268千字　2024年8月北京第1版第2次印刷

购书咨询：010-64518888　　　　　　　　　　　　　售后服务：010-64518899
网　　址：http://www.cip.com.cn
凡购买本书，如有缺损质量问题，本社销售中心负责调换。

定　　价：48.00元　　　　　　　　　　　　　　　　　　　　版权所有　违者必究

《旅游职业英语》编审人员

主　编　刘红梅　李丽萍　李雨桐

副主编　任　露　杨　扬　李梦蝶

编　者（按照姓氏汉语拼音顺序排列）

　　　　程俊梅（青城山六善酒店）

　　　　龚贵尧（四川工商职业技术学院）

　　　　李丽萍（四川工商职业技术学院）

　　　　李梦蝶（四川工商职业技术学院）

　　　　李雨桐（四川工商职业技术学院）

　　　　刘红梅（四川工商职业技术学院）

　　　　任　露（四川工商职业技术学院）

　　　　吴雅秋（成都新希望高新皇冠假日酒店）

　　　　向琼英（四川工商职业技术学院）

　　　　徐　盼（四川工商职业技术学院）

　　　　许玲利（四川工商职业技术学院）

　　　　杨　蔷（四川工商职业技术学院）

　　　　杨　扬（四川工商职业技术学院）

　　　　张　锐（四川工商职业技术学院）

　　　　周　乐（四川工商职业技术学院）

主　审　胡　晓（香港理工大学）

前　言

《旅游职业英语》主要为旅游管理专业群（含导游、酒店管理、空乘）两年或三年制职业院校学生以及想学习旅游英语和从事旅游行业相关工作的社会人员而编写，旨在通过线上、线下的教学和训练，帮助学员较全面、系统地了解旅游行业发展现状，酒店业、旅行社、航空公司等领域的部门组成及对客服务流程，扩展知识面，提升语言素养，增强行业自豪感，同时可以启发学生创新创业兴趣，增知益智，为其从事涉外旅游服务与管理工作打下良好的专业基础。

本教材是以游客的"旅游过程"为主线，串联旅行社、酒店、航空公司相关工作岗位的工作内容和工作流程，以真人拍摄的实际案例模拟旅游行程安排和旅游过程管理。分为概述、出团前工作、导引服务、食宿安排、机场服务、客户关系维护六大模块，共20个单元。具体内容包括：旅游过程中相关岗位的具体工作内容和流程；著名国际酒店集团概况以及旅游行业发展趋势；签证办理相关知识；四川著名景点的英文讲解；旅游活动六大要素"吃、住、行、游、购、娱"的常用英语词汇和旅游行业的英语专有名词；旅行社、机场、酒店、景点游览、餐厅、娱乐场所、免税店等不同情境下旅游接待的常用英语交际表达方式；酒店预订单、客房登记单、洗衣单、通告、菜单、旅游计划安排等旅游文案的写作等。

本教材在内容编排上设计成闭合环线，从旅游者出发前的行程讨论－旅游实施－旅游归途－后期跟进（客户档案建立），通过学习，初涉旅游行业的读者能对整个旅游过程有整体把握。教材侧重听力和口语训练，以增强读者英语学习的信心；阅读部分主要介绍行业相关动态、有代表性的旅游企业以及四川省内的著名景点，以拓展学员知识面和英语词汇量。书中配有65个同步真人视频和音频，以展示口头语言和肢体语言对客的礼仪礼貌，有效提升其英语对客服务能力。

本教材由四川工商职业技术学院的刘红梅、李丽萍、李雨桐老师担任主编，任露、杨扬、李梦蝶老师担任副主编，参与教材编写的还有向琼英、龚贵尧、杨蔷、徐盼、周乐、许玲利、张锐、吴雅秋、程俊梅老师。其中，刘红梅老师负责 module 1 和 module 4 两大模块的编写，李丽萍老师负责 module 3 模块的编写，李雨桐老师负责 module 2 模块的编写，任露和李梦蝶老师负责 module 5 模块的编写，杨扬老师负责 module 6 模块的编写，向琼英、龚贵尧老师参与编写了 module 4，杨蔷老师参与编写了 module 2，徐盼、周乐老师参与编写了 module 3，许玲利老师参与编写了 module 5，张锐老师参与编写了 module 6 并负责全书的初稿排版和格式订正，吴雅秋总监、程俊梅总监参与编写了 module 4。

  本教材由香港理工大学酒店管理博士胡晓主审。胡博士认真阅读研究了本书稿，并提出修改和审阅意见，对编者是极好的教益。另外，本书还得到了旅游行业诸多专家和专业人士的大力帮助和支持，并参考了同行专家的国内外著作和研究成果，在此一并表示衷心的感谢。

  由于编者水平有限，书中难免有疏漏之处，敬请广大专家和读者批评指正。

编 者

2020 年 5 月

目 录
CONTENTS

Module 1   Introduction **001**

    Unit 1   English Phonetic symbols 002

Module 2   Pre-travel **007**

    Unit 2   Tour Consultation 008
    Unit 3   Visa Processing 015
    Unit 4   Tour Reservation 030
    Unit 5   Tour Arrangement 035

Module 3   Tour Guide Service **041**

    Unit 6   Travel Introduction 042
    Unit 7   Check in at the Airport 048
    Unit 8   National Guide 055
    Unit 9   Local Guide 063

Module 4   Hotel accommodation **071**

    Unit 10   Check in 072
    Unit 11   F & B Service 083
    Unit 12   Housekeeping Service 092
    Unit 13   Check out 100

Module 5   Airport Service **109**

    Unit 14   Seeing-off service 110
    Unit 15   Baggage Check-in 120

Unit 16　Duty-free Shopping 128
Unit 17　In-flight Service 136

Module 6　Customer Relationship Management 147

Unit 18　Calling for Feedback 148
Unit 19　Dealing with Complaints 155
Unit 20　Information Service 162

参考文献 168

Module 1
Introduction

Unit 1 | English Phonetic symbols

 Learning objectives

1. Know the differences between K.K and DJ.
2. Master the correct pronunciation of the phonetic symbols and syllables.
3. Know how to divide the words into syllables.

Part I | Warming up

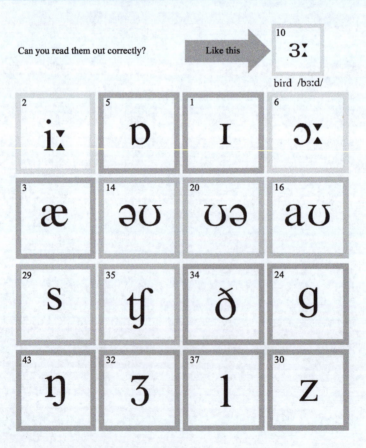

"We may encounter many defeats but we must not be defeated."
（我们可能会遭遇很多失败，但我们绝不能被打败。）

——Maya Angelou

Part II Reading

Going Places: Chinese Tourism

On May 22, 2019, ITB China, the country's largest travel trade show, opens in Shanghai. China is the world's fastest-growing major source of tourists. It is estimated that 160m Chinese will take foreign trips next year, spending a combined $315bn. All that flying abroad on holiday means that China will overtake America as the world's biggest aviation market by 2022, predicts the International Air Transport Association, a trade group.

However, some Western travel firms have struggled to board the Chinese tourism gravy plane. Recent research from McKinsey, a consultancy, suggests a reason for this. Contrary to Western stereotypes, Chinese tourists dislike foreign holidays that involve going around in tour groups, only visiting the most famous landmarks, and on which the only food available is Chinese. It turns out that when they go abroad, they want something different from what they can get at home.

After reading, please answer the questions below:
1. What is predicted by the International Air Transport Association?
2. Why is it difficult for some Western travel firms to board the Chinese tourism gravy plane?

Part III Listening

Listen and circle the English phonetic symbols you hear.

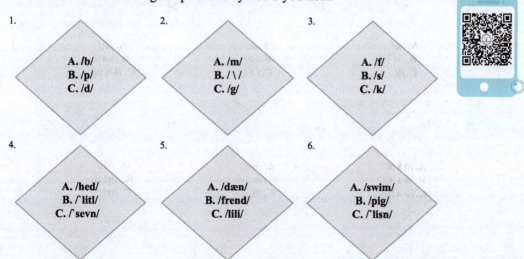

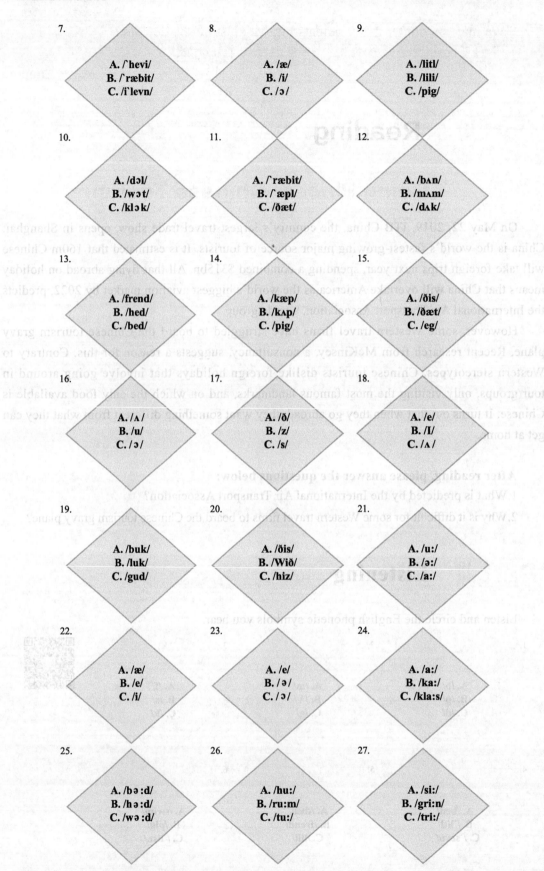

Module 1 Introduction   005

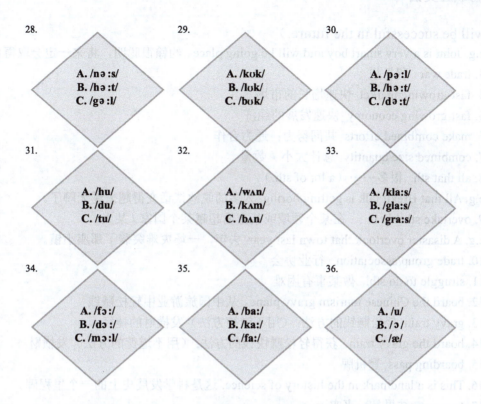

Part IV Vocabulary & Notes

Textbook	Word stress	Translation
trade	TRADE	交易，贸易；行业
fast-growing	FAST-growing	快速增长的
estimate	ES-ti-mate	估计
gauge	GAUGE	估计；测算（常常会涉及到用精确的工具来测量）
combined	com-BINED	总计的，合计的；联合的
overtake	o-ver-TAKE	赶超；某事（不好的事）突然降临到某人／某个地方
predict	pre-DICT	预测；预计（根据经验或知识对未来做出预测）
gravy	GRA-vy	肉汁
board	BOARD	登机；登船
consultancy	con-SUL-tan-cy	咨询公司
stereotype	STE-re-o-type	刻板印象
landmark	LAND-mark	地标；里程碑

Notes

1. go places 旅游（travel）
2. be going places 某人未来会成功 (Someone shows a lot of ability or talent

and will be successful in the future.)

  e.g. John is a very smart boy and will be going places. 约翰很聪明，将来一定会取得成功。

 3. trade war 贸易战

 4. fast-growing market 快速增长的市场

 5. fast-growing economy 快速发展的经济

 6. make combined efforts 共同努力；通力合作

 7. combined size/quantity 总计大小 / 数量

 8. all that sth. 很多……（a lot of sth.）

  e.g. All that Brexit talk is getting boring. 太多的脱欧谈话变得越来越无聊了。

 9. overtake sth./sb. in … 在某个领域或某方面超越某个国家 / 某人

  e.g. A disaster overtook that town last year. 去年，一场灾难突袭了那座小镇。

 10. trade group/association 行业协会

 11. struggle to do sth. 做某事有困难

 12. board the Chinese tourism gravy plane 从中国旅游业中轻松赚钱

 13. gravy train 轻松赚钱的方法；（用不道德方法）发横财的捷径

 14. board the gravy train 获得轻松赚快钱的方法；（用不道德的方法）发横财

 15. boarding pass 登机牌

 16. This is a landmark in the history of science. 这是科学发展史上的一个里程碑。

 17. turn out 结果是；事实上

阅读译文

未来可期：中国旅游业

  2019年5月22日，中国最大的旅游交易展会ITB China在上海开幕。中国是世界上增速最快的主要客源市场。2020年，预计将有1.6亿中国民众出国旅游，总计消费达3150亿美元。据行业协会国际航空运输协会预测，这么多游客假期飞往国外，意味着到2022年，中国将一举超越美国成为世界最大的航空市场。

  不过，一些西方旅游公司想从中国旅游市场分一杯羹却没那么容易。我们或许可以从咨询公司麦肯锡最近的研究中窥见个中原因。与西方的刻板印象相反，出国度假的中国游客对跟着旅游团到处走走停停并不感兴趣，因为这些旅游团只带他们去最有名的景点打卡，吃的也都是中餐。实际上，他们出国想得到的是一些国内所没有的体验。

Part V Discussion

 1. How to learn Tourism Professional English well?

 2. Compare the differences between Tourism Professional English and College Public English?

Module 2
Pre-travel

Unit 2 | Tour Consultation

Learning objectives

1. Know the names and logos about the famous travel agencies.
2. Master the useful expressions about the travel agency.
3. Know the development of the travel agency and the modern tourism industry.

Part I | Warming up

Can you recognize the logo of each travel agency?

_____ _____ _____ _____

_____ _____ _____ _____

"There is always room at the top."
（无限风光在险峰。）

——Daniel Webster, Statesman

Part II Reading

The production and development of the first travel agent in foreign countries

The emergence of foreign travel agencies originated from the industrial revolution. Since Thomas Cook founded the first commercial travel agency, foreign travel agencies have begun a vigorous development process.

In the middle of the 18th century, the industrial revolution occurred in Britain, which spread rapidly to France, Germany and other European countries and North America. In the middle of the 19th century, the industrial revolution made great progress in these countries and regions. It made significant changes in its economic and social structure, which provided various favorable necessary conditions for the emergence of the travel agency industry.

With the rapid development of productive forces and the rapid increase of social wealth, the scale of the proletariat is expanding day by day, so people in the developed countries of Europe and the United States have can take advantage of the economic conditions to travel. Before the Industrial Revolution, only landlords and aristocrats had the financial power to engage in non-economic recreational tourism. After the industrial revolution, plenty of wealth went to the new industrial bourgeoisie, so that they also had the economic conditions to engage in tourism, which expanded the flow of people traveling.

Secondly, with the progress of science and technology, especially the significant development of transportation technology. Transportation capacity is improved, the transportation time is shortened, the large-scale personnel flow becomes possible, and people travel convenient. In 1769 Watt invented the steam engine technology, which soon became a new vehicle. By the end of the 18th century, the steam engine ship came out. After that, the railway transport had been produced again, which had the most direct influence on the birth of modern tourism. In 1825, the UK's parent of the rail George Stevenson-built Stopton-Darlington railway was officially put into operation. After that, railway began to be built and developed everywhere.

Thirdly, the industrial revolution accelerated the process of urbanization and shifted the focus of people's work and life from rural to urban. This change has finally led to the need to escape the rhythmic urban life and crowded and noisy environmental pressure at the right time, resulting in the upsurge of returning to freedom and nature.

Finally, the industrial revolution changed the nature of people's work. With the rapid development of the industrial revolution, the number of people from rural manual workers to urban workers had increased. Then a large number of people poured into the city, resulting in strong holiday requirements. Workers hoped to return to nature and enjoy temporary freedom, which was the initial tourism motivation. Although the paid holidays of the working class were obtained after more than a century of hard struggle, they were successful. However, people lack knowledge and experience of tourism, which requires professional tourism services. In this series of background conditions, the world's first travel agency was born. Thomas Cook, an Englishman, was the first to observe that the booming demand for tourism gave birth to tremendous business opportunities. Thomas Cook founded Thomas Cook Travel Service in his hometown of Leicester in 1845. Since then, he has become the first full-time travel agent in the world and has been praised by future generations as the "father of modern tourism." In the summer of the same year, he organized a sightseeing trip from Lester to Liverpool for the first time.

It was a commercial, profit-making organization that took several days, Thomas Cook himself the tour group was accompanied and guide by a local tour guide during his stay in Wales. In order to facilitate visitors to understand the whole process, Thomas Cook specially organized the preparation of a Liverpool tour manual. It shows that Thomas Cook has begun to explore and establish the business model of travel agencies.

In 1865, he founded Thomas Cook and his son. Thomas Cook is recognized as the ancestor of modern tourism and travel agencies, and Thomas Cook Company, which he founded, is still a well-known travel agency brand enterprise in the world.

After the reading please answer the questions below:
1. What happen the industrial revolution in 19th century?
2. What impact did the industrial revolution have on modern tourism?
3. Who is the founder of the first travel agency?
4. When and where did he found the first travel agency?

Part Ⅲ Listening

Listen to *dialogues* and finish the tasks.
Situational dialogue 1
Context: Carol is a staff of the travel agency; she is helping Eric and his friend David to make a travel plan.
Task: answer the questions below.
1. What are they talking about?
2. Where is this conversation happening?

Carol: Good morning, welcome to Mingjiang travel agency. May I help you?
Eric: Good morning, we're planning to travel to China, so we want to consult something.
Carol: Sure, come in and have a seat, please.
Eric: Thanks!
Carol: What would you like to drink?
David: Coffee.

Eric: Two cups of coffee then, please.

Carol: Please wait for a moment, I will come back soon with your coffee and some travel information.

Eric: Ok, sure, thank you.

Carol: It's my pleasure.

Situational dialogue 2

Context: Carol is a staff of the travel agency; he is helping Eric and his friend David to make a travel plan.

Task: answer the questions below.

1. What are they talking about?
2. Why don't they want to go to Wuhan?
3. Where they finally decided to go?

Carol: Good morning, here is our travel itinerary information, please have a look.

Eric: OK, thank you.

Carol: Where do you want to go?

David: We are not sure. We want to travel to China, but we don't know which city is the better choice for us, so I hope you can give us some advice.

Carol: Of course, I am willing to do that!

Eric: Thank you!

Carol: OK. China has so many cities, which city do you like best? How about Wuhan, I think there are so many sightseeing in Wuhan.

Eric: I don't like Wuhan. Wuhan is too crowd.

Carol: OK, It's doesn't matter. How about Chengdu?

David: I think it's a good idea!

Eric: Well, you know that saying 'Chengdu is famous for its spicy food'. In general, Chengdu is a leisure city with a mild climate. The people there are very hospitable and speak the authentic Sichuan dialect.

Eric: I think it is a good choice.

David: I think so.

Carol: Let me try to summarize here. You want to go to Chengdu, right?

Eric: Yes.

Carol: Ok. we will make an itinerary later and then you can see if you are okay with it.

Eric: Thank you very much!

Carol: It's my pleasure, if you have any questions, just ask me for help.

Situational dialogue 3

Context: Carol is a staff of Mingjiang travel agency, he is helping Eric and David make traveling plan to Chengdu.

Tasks: answer the questions below.
1. When will they arrive in Chengdu?
2. How days they will stay in Dujiangyan?
3. Which hotel will they stay during the visiting in Dujiangyan?

Carol: Hello, we have an itinerary in Chengdu.The attractions around, the trip is as follows. First, go sightseeing in Chengdu for 3 days, and then go to Dujiangyan to visit the Dujiangyan Irrigation System, and Mt.Qingcheng, and finally get our way to Jiuzhaigou where it's famous for the natural landscape.

Eric: That sounds good, and how long is the total journey?

Carol: 9 days, we will arrive in Chengdu 18th of September.

Eric: So how about the hotel?

Carol: All the hotel in this itinerary are five-star hotels. For example, we will stay in Jinjiang hotel in Chengdu, which is the one of the most famous hotel in Chengdu with a long history, and is located in the city center, then during the visit to Dujiangyan, we'll stay in the Six Sense hotel in Mt.Qingcheng.

Eric: That is perfect. How much is this journey in total?

Carol: 2600 euro per person, including all the things.

Eric: I think it's good, we'll take this itinerary.

Carol: OK, let me print the itinerary information for you and may I have your passport please?

Eric: Here you are.

Carol: Thank you, please wait for a moment.(a few minutes later) Here is your passport and your contract, two people to Chengdu on 18th of September, please confirm your information, if it's all right, please sign here.

Eric: OK, I think its alright.

Carol: Here is your contract, and we'll send you the confirmation as soon as possible, and we also have the staff to help you to do the visa things, hotel reservation...and so on, so if you have any questions, please do not hesitate to contact us.

Eric: Thank you so much.

Carol: You're welcome.

Part IV Vocabulary

Textbook	Word stress	Translation
emergence	e-MER-gen-ce	出现，浮现
vigorous	VI-go-rous	有力的；精力充沛的
original	o-RI-gi-nal	原来的；开始的；原始的
Travel agency	A-gen-cy	旅行社
industrial	in-DAS-trial	工业的；产业的

Textbook	Word stress	Translation
revolution	re-vo-LU-tion	革命
European	euro-PEAN	欧洲的；欧洲人的
recreational	re-cre-A-tional	娱乐的；消遣的
urbanization	ur-ba-ni-ZA-tion	都市化
rhythmic	RHY-th-mic	有节奏的
expand	ex-PAND	扩张；使膨胀
Sightseeing	SIGH-t-see-ing	观光；游览
rural	RU-ral	农村的；乡下的
temporary	TEM-po-ra-ry	暂时的
ancestor	AN-ces-tor	祖先
enterprise	EN-ter-pri-se	企业
manual	MA-nu-al	体力的；手控的；用手的

阅读译文

国外第一家旅行社的产生和发展

国外旅行社的产生起源于产业革命，自从托马斯·库克创办了第一家商业旅行社，国外的旅行社便开始了蓬勃的发展历程。

18世纪中叶，英国开始了工业革命，这一革命迅速影响到法国、德国等欧洲国家和北美地区。19世纪中叶，工业革命在这些国家和地区取得了重大进展，并促使其经济结构和社会结构发生了巨大的变化，这为旅行社行业的产生提供了各种有利的基础条件。

首先，随着生产力的迅速发展和社会财富的急剧增加，工人阶级的规模日趋扩大。因此欧美发达国家的人们具备了外出旅游的经济条件。工业革命以前，只有地主和贵族才有财力从事以非经济为目的的消遣旅游活动。工业革命开始后，财富大量流向了新兴的工业中产阶级，使得他们也具备了旅游的经济条件，这便扩大了外出旅游的人数。

其次，随着科学技术的进步，特别是交通运输技术的大力发展，提高了运输能力，缩短了运输时间，使得大规模的人员流动成为可能，人们出行变得方便了。1769年瓦特发明的蒸汽机技术，很快便被应用于新的交通工具。到了18世纪末，蒸汽机轮船问世了。之后，铁路运输又产生了，它对近代旅游业的诞生影响最大也最直接。1825年，英国享有"铁路之父"之称的乔治·史蒂文森建造的斯托克顿至达林顿的铁路正式投入运营。此后，各地的铁路逐渐建设并发展起来了。

再次，工业革命加速了城市化的进程，使人们工作和生活的重心从农村转移到城市。这变化最终导致人们产生了适时逃避节奏紧张的城市生活和拥挤嘈杂的环境压力的需求，出现了回归自由、回归大自然的热潮。

最后，工业革命改变了人们的工作性质。随着工业革命的迅速发展，从农村体力劳动者转变为城市工人的人数越来越多，进而大量人群涌入城市，致使人们产生了强烈的度假需求。工人们盼望能够回归大自然、享受短暂的自由，这便是最初的旅游动机。虽然，工人阶级的带薪假日是经过一个多世纪的艰苦斗争才得来的，但还是成功了。但人们缺乏旅游知识和经验，这就需要专业化的旅游机构为其提供服务。

在这一系列的背景条件下，世界上第一家旅行社诞生了。英国人托马斯·库克最先敏锐地观察到，蓬勃发展的旅游需求孕育着巨大的商机。1845年托马斯·库克在他的家乡莱斯特成立了托马斯·库克旅行社。从此，他成为了世界上第一位专职的旅行代理商，被后人誉为"近代旅游业之父"。同年夏天，他首次组织了从莱斯特到利物浦的观光旅游。

这是一次商业性的、以营利为目的的组织活动，而且耗时数日，托马斯·库克亲自担任该旅行团的陪同和导游，在威尔士停留期间，他还聘用了地方导游。为了便于游客了解全程活动的安排情况，托马斯·库克特意组织编写了一本《利物浦之行手册》。这表明，托马斯·库克已经开始探索并建立旅行社的业务模式。

1865年，他创办了托马斯·库克父子公司。托马斯·库克被公认为近代旅游业和旅行社的鼻祖，而他创立的托马斯·库克公司，至今仍是国际上知名度很高的旅行社品牌企业。

Part V　Discussion

1. What did you learn from this unit?
2. Consult and tell the history of another travel agency.
3. Suppose you are a staff in the travel agency, you have received a group of 18 foreign travelers. How to help them with the tour route?

Part VI　Writing

According to what you have learned in this unit, try to make a tour route about taking the foreign travelers to visit the Irrigation system of Dujiangyan.

Unit 3 Visa Processing

  Learning objectives

1. Know the process about how to apply the visa.
2. Master the useful expressions about visa processing.

Part I Warming up

Question: Can you name at least ten countries that have visa-free access to China?

"Strength alone knows conflict, weakness is below even defeat, and is born vanquished."
（只有强者才知道冲突，弱者甚至比失败还要弱，生来就是被征服的。）
—Swetchine

Part II Reading

Chinese Visa system

What is the primary purpose of your visit to China and which is the most appropriate visa category for your application?

Categories Description of Visa

Visa Categories	Description of Visa
C	Issued to foreign crew members of means of international transportation, including aircraft, trains and ships, or motor vehicle drivers engaged in cross-border transport activities, or to the accompanying family members of the crew members of the above-mentioned ships.
D	Issued to those who intend to reside in China permanently.
F	Issued to those who intend to go to China for exchanges, visits, study toursand other activities.
G	Issued to those who intend to transit through China.
J1	Issued to resident foreign journalists of foreign news organizations stationed in China. The intended duration of stay in China exceeds 180 days.
J2	Issued to foreign journalists who intend to go to China for short-term news coverage. The intended duration of stay in China is no more than 180 days.
L	Issued to those who intend to go to China as a tourist.
M	Issued to those who intend to go to China for commercial and trade activities.
Q1	Issued to those who are family members of Chinese citizens or of foreigners with Chinese permanent residence and intend to go to China for family reunion, or to those who intend to go to China for the purpose of foster care. The intended duration of stay in China exceeds 180 days. "Family members" refers to spouses, parents, sons, daughters, spouses of sons or daughters, brothers, sisters, grandparents, grandsons, granddaughters and parents-in-law.
Q2	Issued to those who intend to visit their relatives who are Chinese citizens residing in China or foreigners with permanent residence in China. The intended duration of stay in China is no more than 180 days.
R	Issued to those who are high-level talents or whose skills are urgently needed in China.
S1	Issued to those who intend to go to China to visit the foreigners working or studying in China to whom they are spouses, parents, sons or daughters under the age of 18 or parents-in-law, or to those who intend to go to China for other private affairs. The intended duration of stay in China exceeds 180 days.
S2	Issued to those who intend to visit their family members who are foreigners working or studying in China, or to those who intend to go to China for other private matters. The intended duration of stay in China is no more than 180 days. "family members" refers to spouses, parents, sons, daughters, spouses of sons or daughters, brothers, sisters, grandparents, grandsons, granddaughters and parents-in-law.
X1	Issued to those who intend to study in China for a period of more than 180 days.
X2	Issued to those who intend to study in China for a period of no more than 180 days.
Z	Issued to those who intend to work in China.

Here are the documents you shall prepare before submission of visa application:

1. Basic Documents

(1) Passport　Original passport with at least six months of remaining validity and blank visa pages, and a photocopy of the passport's data page and the photo page if it is separate.

(2) Visa Application Form and Photo　One completed Visa Application Form with a recently-taken color passport photo (bare-head, full face) against a light background attached.

(3) Proof of legal stay or residence status (applicable to those not applying for the visa in their country of citizenship)　If you are not applying for the visa in the country of your citizenship, you must provide the original and photocopy of your valid certificates or visa of stay, residence, employment or student status, or other valid certificates of legal staying provided by the relevant authorities of the country where you are currently staying.

(4) Photocopy of previous Chinese passports or previous Chinese visas (applicable to foreign citizens those who were Chinese citizens and have obtained foreign citizenship).

If you are applying for a Chinese visa for the first time, you should provide your previous

Chinese passport held and a photocopy of its data page.

If you have obtained Chinese visas before and want to apply for a Chinese visa with a renewed foreign passport that does not contain any Chinese visa, you should present the photocopy of the previous passport's data page and the photo page if it is separate, as well as the previous Chinese visa page. (If your name on the current passport differs from that on the previous one, you must provide an official document of the name change.)

2. Supporting Documents

C-Visa

A letter of guarantee issued by a foreign transport company or an invitation letter issued by a relevant entity in China.

D-Visa

The original and photocopy of the Confirmation Form for Foreigners Permanent Residence Status issued by the Ministry of Public Security of China.

We kindly remind you that:

Holders of D Visa shall, within 30 days from the date of their entry, apply to the exit/entry administrations of public security organs under local people's governments at or above the county level in the proposed places of residence for foreigners' residence permits.

F-Visa

An invitation letter issued by a relevant entity or individual in China. The invitation should contain:

(1) Information on the applicant (full name, gender, date of birth, etc.)

(2) Information on the planned visit [purpose of visit, arrival and departure dates, place(s) to be visited, relations between the applicant and the inviting entity or individual, financial source for expenditures]

(3) Information on the inviting entity or individual (name, contact telephone number, address, official stamp, signature of the legal representative or the inviting individual)

G-Visa

An onward air (train or ship) ticket with confirmed date and seat to the destination country or region.

J1-Visa

Visa Notification Letter issued by the Information Department of the Ministry of Foreign Affairs of China and an official letter issued by the media organization for which the journalist works.

Applicants should contact the press section of the Chinese Embassy/Consulate General in advance or and complete relevant formalities.

We kindly remind you that:

Holders of J1 Visa shall, within 30 days from the date of their entry, apply to the exit/entry administrations of public security organs under local people's governments at or above the county level in the proposed places of residence for foreigners' residence permits.

J2-Visa

Visa Notification Letter issued by the Information Department of the Ministry of Foreign Affairs of China or other authorized units in China and an official letter issued by the media organization for which the journalist works.

Applicants should contact the press section of the Chinese Embassy/Consulate General in advance and complete the required formalities.

L-Visa

Documents showing the itinerary including air ticket booking record (round trip) and proof of a hotel reservation, etc. or an invitation letter issued by a relevant entity or individual in China. The invitation letter should contain:

(1) Information on the applicant (full name, gender, date of birth, etc.)

(2) Information on the planned visit [arrival and departure dates, place(s) to be visited, etc.]

(3) Information on the inviting entity or individual (name, contact telephone number, address, official stamp, signature of the legal representative or the inviting individual)

M-Visa

Documents on the commercial activity issued by a trade partner in China, or trade fair invitation or other invitation letters issued by relevant entity or individual. The invitation letter should contain:

a) Information on the applicant (full name, gender, date of birth, etc.)

b) Information on the planned visit [purpose of visit, arrival and departure dates, place(s) to be visited, relations between the applicant and the inviting entity or individual, financial source for expenditures]

c) Information on the inviting entity or individual (name, contact telephone number, address, official stamp, signature of the legal representative or the inviting individual)

Q1-Visa

For family reunion, the following documents are required:

(1) An invitation letter issued by a Chinese citizen or a foreign citizen with a Chinese permanent residence permit who lives in China. The invitation letter should contain:

a) Information on the applicant (full name, gender, date of birth, etc.)

b) Information on the visit [purpose of visit, intended arrival date, place(s) of intended residence, intended duration of residence, relations between the applicant and the inviting entity or individual, financial source for expenditures]

c) Information on the inviting individual (name, contact telephone number, address, official stamp, signature of legal representative or the inviting individual, etc.)

(2) Photocopy of Chinese ID of the inviting individual or foreign passport and permanent residence permit.

(3) Original and photocopy of certification (marriage certificate, birth certificate, certification of kinship issued by Public Security Bureau or notarized certification of kinship) showing the relationship of family members between applicant and inviting individual.

"Family members" refers to spouses, parents, sons, daughters, spouses of sons or daughters, brothers, sisters, grandparents, grandsons, granddaughters and parents-in-law.

For foster care, the following documents are required:

(1) Foster entrustment notarization issued by Chinese Embassies/Consulates General in foreign countries or Foster Care Power of Attorney notarized and authenticated in the country of residence or in China.

(2) Original and photocopy of the consignor's passport(s), as well as the original and photocopy of certification (marriage certificate, birth certificate, certification of kinship issued by Public Security Bureau or notarized certification of kinship) notarized and authenticated certification showing the relationship between parents or guardians and children.

(3) A letter of consent on foster care issued by the trustee living in China who has agreed to provide foster care services and a photocopy of the ID of the trustee.

(4) A photocopy of the certificate indicating the permanent residence status abroad of the parent(s) when the child was born, provided that either or both parents of the child are Chinese citizens.

We kindly remind you that:

Holders of Q1 Visa shall, within 30 days from the date of their entry, apply to the exit/entry administrations of public security organs under local people's governments at or above the county level in the proposed places of residence for foreigners' residence permits.

Q2-Visa

(1) An invitation letter issued by a Chinese citizen or a foreign citizen with a Chinese permanent residence permit who lives in China. The invitation letter should contain:

a) Information on the applicant (full name, gender, date of birth, etc.)

b) Information on the visit [purpose of visit, arrival and departure dates, place(s) to be visited, relations between the applicant and the inviting individual, financial source for expenditures]

c) Information on the inviting individual (name, contact number, address, signature etc.)

(2) Photocopy of Chinese ID or foreign passport and permanent residence permit of the inviting individual.

R-Visa

The applicant should submit relevant certification in accordance with relevant regulations, and meet the relevant requirements of the competent authorities of the Chinese government on high-level talents and individual with special skills urgently needed by China.

S1-Visa

(1) An invitation letter from the inviting individual (a foreigner who stays or resides in China for work or studies) which contains:

a) Information on the applicant (full name, gender, date of birth, etc.)

b) Information on the visit (purpose of visit, arrival and departure dates, place of intended residence, relations between the applicant and the inviting individual, financial source for expenditures, etc.)

c) Information on the inviting individual (name, contact telephone number, address, signature, etc.)

(2) A photocopy of the inviting individual's passport and residence permit.

(3) Original and photocopy of certification (marriage certificate, birth certificate, certification of kinship issued by Public Security Bureau or notarized certification of kinship) showing the relationship of immediate family members between applicants and inviting individual.

"immediate family members" refers to spouses, parents, sons or daughters under the age of 18, parents-in-law.

We kindly remind you that:

Holders of S1 Visa shall, within 30 days from the date of their entry, apply to the exit/entry administrations of public security organs under local people's governments at or above the county level in the proposed places of residence for foreigners' residence permits.

S2-Visa

For visiting family members for a short period, the following documents are required:

(1) An invitation letter issued by the inviting individual (a foreigner who stays or resides in China for work or studies) which contains:

a) Information on the applicant (full name, gender, date of birth, etc.)

b) Information on the visit (purpose of visit, arrival and departure dates, place(s) to be visited, relations between the applicant and the inviting individual, financial source for expenditures, etc.)

c) Information on the inviting individual (name, contact telephone number, address, signature, etc.)

(2) A photocopy of the inviting individual's (a foreigner who stays or lives in China for work or studies) passport and residence permit.

(3) Photocopy of certification (marriage certificate, birth certificate or notarized certification of kinship) showing the relationship of family members between the applicant and the inviting individual.

"Family members" refers to spouses, parents, sons, daughters, spouses of sons or daughters, brothers, sisters, grandparents, grandsons, granddaughters and parents-in-law.

For private affairs, documentation identifying the nature of the private affairs should be provided as required by the consular officer.

X1-Visa

(1) Original and photocopy of the Admission Letter issued by a school or other entities in China.

(2) Original and photocopy of "Visa Application for Study in China" (Form JW201 or Form JW202).

We kindly remind you that:

Holders of X1 Visa shall, within 30 days from the date of their entry, apply to the exit/entry administrations of public security organs under local people's governments at or above the county level in the proposed places of residence for foreigners' residence permits.

X2-Visa

Original and photocopy of Admission Notice issued by a school or other entities in China.

Z-Visa

One of the following documents:

(1) Foreigners Employment Permit of the People's Republic of China issued by Chinese government authorities for Human Resources and Social Security, as well as Invitation Letter of Duly Authorized Entity or Confirmation Letter of Invitation issued by relevant Chinese entities.

(2) Permit for Foreign Experts Working in China issued by the State Bureau of Foreign Experts as well as Invitation Letter of Duly Authorized Entity or Confirmation Letter of Invitation issued by relevant Chinese entities.

(3) Registration Certificate of Resident Representative Offices of enterprises of foreign countries(regions) issued by Chinese authorities of industrial and commercial administration, as well as Invitation Letter of Duly Authorized Entity or Confirmation Letter of Invitation issued by relevant Chinese entities as well as Invitation Letter of Duly Authorized Entity or Confirmation Letter of Invitation issued by relevant Chinese entities.

(4) An approval document for commercial performances issued by the Chinese government authorities for cultural affairs or Invitation Letter of Duly Authorized Entity or Confirmation Letter of Invitation issued by relevant Foreign Affairs Office of provincial governments of China.

(5) Letter of Invitation to Foreigners for Offshore Petroleum Operations in China issued by China National Offshore Oil Corporation;

We kindly remind you that:

Holders of Z Visa shall, within 30 days from the date of their entry, apply to the exit/entry administrations of public security organs under local people's governments at or above the county level in the proposed places of residence for foreigners' residence permits.

3. Special Reminder

(1) The invitation letter may be in the form of fax, photocopy or computer printout, but the consular officer may require the applicant to submit the original of the invitation letter.

(2) If necessary, the consular officer may require the applicant to provide other proof documents or supplementary materials, or require an interview with the applicant.

(3) The consular officer will decide on whether or not to issue the visa and on its validity, duration of stay and number of entries in light of specific conditions of the applicant.

(4) For further details, please visit the web-site of the relevant Chinese Embassy or Consulate General.

After the reading please answer the questions below:

1. If a tourist want to travel to China, when should he apply the visa before his departure?
2. What should a tourist prepare if he want to apply the Chinese visa?

Part III Listening

Listen to *dialogues* and finish the tasks.

Situational dialogue 1

Context: Visa consulting: Sherry is a staff in Mingjiang travel agency, and she has the responsibilities for the visa process of Eric and David's journey.

Task: answer the question below.

1. What should Eric and David do during this period?
2. Why did Sherry ask them to come to office to talk face to face?

Sherry: Good morning, this is Mingjiang travel agency, my name is Sherry, I saw your travel plan to Chengdu, China, i will help you and your friend to apply for the visa.

Eric: Morning Sherry.

Sherry: You will travel in September, right?

Eric: Yes!

Sherry: Fine, is has months left, so you have enough time to prepare.

Eric: That's great! So what should we do for the preparation?

Sherry: Emmm, I think it is better to talk face to face, because you should prepare so many files, so do you have time to our office to consult?

Eric: Sure, I will come tomorrow.

Sherry: That is great, we are looking forward to seeing you.

Eric: Thank you, bye.

Shery: My pleasure.

Situational dialogue 2

Context: Eric is in the travel agency office asking for the information about visa.

Task: answer the question below.

1. Who will help them to apply for the visa?
2. What should they prepare to apply for the visa?

Sherry: Good morning, welcome to Mingjiang travel agency office, I am Sherry, may I help you?

Eric: Hello Sherry, I'm Eric who talked with you on the phone yesterday.

Sherry: Oh yes, nice to meet you, have a seat please.

Eric: Thank you.

Sherry: There are all the information for applying the visa of China, first you should fill in this form, for example, your personal information, your purpose of this trip...etc.

Eric: Let me see.

Sherry: And then, you also need to prepare your photo, the reservation form of your hotel and your flight reservation we'll prepare them for you.

Eric: OK.

Sherry: After those things, you need to make a reservation online and go to the embassy to apply for your visa.

Eric: How can I make a reservation?

Sherry: Don't worry, we can offer you service about this. we can make it for you, and I will accompany you to the embassy.

Eric: That will be great.

Sherry: If you need help, you can call us anytime.

Eric: OK, thank you.

Sherry: You're welcome. If you have any questions, please feel free to contact us.

Situational dialogue 3

Context: Eric is filling the application form at home, but he meet some questions, so he is calling the office on the phone for help.

Task: answer the question below.

1. Why did Eric made this call?
2. When will they go to the embassy in this month?

1.1 外文姓名 / Full Name: 姓 / Surname : 中间名 / Middle Name:		照片 /Photo
名 / Given Name :	1.2 性别 / Sex: 男 / M　女 /F	请将1张近期正面免冠、浅色背景的彩色护照照片粘贴于此。 *Please affix one recent passport style color photo, with full face, front view, no hat, and against a plain light background.*
1.3 中文姓名 /Chinese Name if Applicable:	1.4 现有国籍 / Current Nationality:	
1.5 别名或曾用名 / Other or Former Name:	1.6 曾有国籍 /Former Nationality:	
1.7 出生日期 / Date of Birth(YY-MM-DD):	1.8 出生地点 (国、省 / 市) / Place (Province/State, Country) of Birth:	
1.9 护照种类 Passport Type	外交 / Diplomatic 公务、官员 / Service or Official 普通 / Regular 其他证件 (请说明) / Other (Please specify):	
1.10 护照号码 / PassportNumber:	1.11 签发日期 / Date of Issue(YY-MM-DD):	
1.12 签发地点 (省 / 市及国家) / Place (Province/State, Country) of Issue:	1.13 失效日期 / Expiration Date(YY-MM-DD):	
1.14 当前职业（可多选）/ Your Current Occupation(s): 商人 / Businessman　　　　教师、学生 / Teacher or Student　　　　政府官员 / Government Official 乘务人员 / Crew Member of Airlines, Trains or Ships　　　　新闻从业人员 / Staff of Media 议员 / Member of Parliament, Congressman or Senator　　　　宗教人士 / Clergy 其他 (请说明) /Other (Please specify):		

Sherry: Hello, good morning, this is Mingjiang travel agency, what can I do for you?

Eric: Hello, this is Eric, I have no idea how to fill the application form, so could please fill it for me?

Sherry: Ok, sure, please give me your personal information.

Eric: My name is Enic, passport number is E35268719.

Sherry: OK, how about your nationality?

Eric: American.

Sherry: Your date of birth and birth place?

Eric: 30th of June, 1987 in New York.

Sherry: Wait a moment. I'm filling it. And what do you do?

Eric: I am a teacher.

Sherry: So how long you will stay in China and what your purpose of this trip?

Eric: For 9 days, just travel.

Sherry: fine, that's OK. Please confirm your information again, your name is...

Eric: That's all right, thank you very much.

Sherry: You're welcome. By the way, your date for the visa is confirmed at 16th of this month, 9:00 in the morning, please make sure that all the things are prepared well before that day.

Eric: No problem. You'll company us to the embassy right?

Sherry: Yes, sure.

Eric: Thank you so much.

Sherry: You're welcome, see you that day.

Part IV Vocabulary

Textbook	Word stress	Translation
appropriate	a-PPRO-pri-ate	适当的
category	CA-te-go-ry	种类
application	a-ppli-CA-tion	应用；申请
permanent	PER-ma-nent	永久的
issue	I-ssue	问题
journalist	JOUR-na-list	新闻工作者
validity	va-LI-di-ty	有效期
citizen	CI-ti-zen	公民；市民；老百姓
authority	au-THO-ri-ty	权威；权利
previous	PRE-vious	以前的；早先的
residence	RE-si-den-ce	住宅；住处
individual	in-di-VI-dual	个人的；个别的
relevant	RE-le-vant	相关的

Textbook	Word stress	Translation
In advance	IN ad-VAN-ce	提前
signature	SIG-na-ture	签名
entrustment	en-TRUST-ment	委托；信托

阅读译文

中国签证制度

您访问中国的主要目的是什么？最适合您的申请的签证类别是哪一种？

签证类别描述

签证类别	签证说明
C	发给国际运输工具的外国船员，包括从事跨境运输活动的飞机、火车和船舶或者机动车驾驶员，或者发给承运人及上述船舶船员的家属
D	发给有意在中国永久居住的人
F	发给有意来华进行交流、参观、考察等活动的人
G	发给打算过境中国的人
J1	发给驻外新闻机构的常驻外国记者。在中国的预定逗留期限超过180天
J2	发给打算到中国进行短期新闻报道的外国记者。在中国的预定逗留期限不超过180天
L	发给那些打算去中国旅游的人
M	发给有意到中国从事商业贸易活动的人
Q1	发给那些是中国公民的家庭成员或有中国永久居留权的外国人，并打算去中国进行家庭团聚的人，或打算去中国以寄养的目的人。在中国的预定逗留期限超过180天。 "家庭成员"是指配偶、父母、儿子、女儿、儿子或女儿的配偶、兄弟、姐妹、祖父母、孙子、孙女和岳父母
Q2	发给有意探望在中国居住的中国公民或在中国常住的外国人的亲属。在中国的预定逗留期限不超过180天
R	发放给在中国急需的高层次人才或技能人才
S1	发给有意来华访问在中国工作或学习的外国人，如其配偶、父母、未满18周岁的儿子或女儿、岳父母，或者本人打算去中国处理其他私人事务。在中国的预定逗留期限超过180天
S2	发给有意探望在中国工作或学习的外国人家庭成员的，或者打算到中国办理其他私事的人。在中国的预定逗留期限不超过180天 "家庭成员"是指配偶、父母、儿子、女儿、儿子或女儿的配偶、兄弟、姐妹、祖父母、孙子、孙女和岳父母
X1	发给拟在中国学习180天以上的人员
X2	发给拟在中国留学的人员，期限不超过180天
Z	发给有意在中国工作的人员

签证类别说明及其材料
以下是你在递交签证申请前应准备的文件：

1. 基本文件

（1）护照 护照原件（有效期至少6个月、含空白签证页），护照数据页和照片页的复印件(如果是分开的)。

（2）签证申请表及照片 一张已填妥的签证申请表，附有一张最近于浅色背景下拍摄的彩色护照照片。

（3）合法居留或居留身份证明(适用于未在其国籍国申请签证的人) 如果您未在您的国籍国家申请签证，您必须提供您的有效证件（居住证明、就业证明或学生身份签证的原件和复印件，或其他由您目前居住国家的有关当局提供的有效的合法居留证明）。

（4）之前的中国护照或者之前的中国签证的复印件(适用于已取得外国国籍的外国公民)。

如果您是第一次申请中国签证，您需要提供您以前持有的护照及其资料页的复印件。

如果您以前取得过中国签证，并且想用不含中国签证的外国护照申请中国签证，您需要出示之前护照的数据页和照片页的复印件(如果是分开的)，以及以前的中国签证页面(如果当前护照上的姓名与上一本护照上的姓名不同，则必须提供更改姓名的正式文件)。

2. 佐证文件

C- 签证

由外国运输公司出具的保函或中国有关单位发出的邀请信。

D- 签证

由中国公安部颁发的"外国人永久居留身份确认书"的正本及复印件。

我们谨提醒您：

D签证持有人应当自入境之日起30日内向县级以上地方人民政府公安机关申请出入境管理。

F- 签证

由中国有关单位或个人发出的邀请函。邀请应包括：

（1）申请人的资料(全名、性别、出生日期等)。

（2）关于计划访问的资料(访问目的、抵达和离开日期、访问地点、申请人与邀请实体或个人之间的关系、资金来源)。

（3）邀请实体或个人的信息（名称、联系电话、地址、公章、法定代表人或邀请个人签字）。

G- 签证

前往目的地国家或地区的机票(火车或轮船票)，有确定的日期和座位。

J1- 签证

由中国外交部新闻司出具的签证通知函和媒体机构为该记者工作所出具的公函。

申请人应事先与中国大使馆/总领事馆新闻组联系，并完成相关手续。

我们谨提醒您：

J1签证持有人应当自入境之日起30日内向县级以上地方人民政府公安机关办理出入境手续。

J2- 签证

由中国外交部或其他授权单位信息部签发的签证通知书和媒体组织为记者工作所签发的正式信函。申请人应事先与中国大使馆/总领事馆新闻组联系，并完成所需的手续。

L- 签证

列明行程的文件，包括机票预订记录(往返)、酒店预订证明等，或由中国有关单位或个人出具的邀请信。这份邀请函应包括：

（1）申请人的资料(全名、性别、出生日期等)。
（2）关于计划访问的信息（到达和出发日期、待访问地点等）。
（3）邀请实体或个人的信息（名称、联系电话、地址、公章、法定代表人或邀请个人签字）。

M- 签证

由中国贸易伙伴出具的商业活动文件，或者有关单位或个人出具的交易会邀请函或其他邀请函。邀请函应包含：

a）申请人的资料(全名、性别、出生日期等)
b）关于计划访问的资料(访问目的、抵达和离开日期、访问地点、申请人与邀请实体或个人之间的关系、资金来源)
c）关于邀请单位或个人的信息（名称、联系电话、地址、公章、法定代表人或邀请人的签名）

Q1- 签证

家庭团聚需提供下列文件：

（1）由中国公民或者持有中国永久居留证的外国公民发出的邀请函。邀请函应包括：

a）申请人的资料(全名、性别、出生日期等)
b）关于访问的资料(访问目的、预定抵达日期、预定居住地点、预定居住期限、与申请人之间的关系和邀请的实体或个人、资金来源)
c）有关受邀人士的资料(姓名、联络电话、地址、公章、法定代表人或受邀人士的签署等)

（2）被邀请的个人或外国护照和永久居留许可证的复印件。
（3）证书原件和复印件(结婚证、出生证明、由公安局出具的亲属证明或者亲属关系公证)。申请人与受邀个人之间的家庭成员关系。

"家庭成员"是指配偶、父母、儿子、女儿、子女的配偶、兄弟姐妹、祖父母、孙子、孙女和岳父母。

寄养需要下列文件：

（1）中国驻外国使领馆出具的寄养委托公证，或者在居住国或者两地经公证认证的寄养委托书。
（2）寄养发出人的护照原件和复印件，以及公证(结婚证书、出生证、亲属证明)原件和复印件。对父母或监护人与子女之间的关系进行公证和认证。
（3）已同意提供寄养服务及受托人身份影印件的中国受托人就寄养所发出的寄养服务的同意书。
（4）子女出生时父母一方或双方均为中国公民的证明文件的复印本。

我们谨提醒您：
Q1签证持有人自入境之日起30日内，适用于县级以上地方人民政府公安机关出入境管理部门 外国人居留许可的居住地点。

Q2- 签证

（1）中国公民或者持有中国永久居留证的外国公民发出的邀请函。邀请函应包括：

a）申请人的资料(全名、性别、出生日期等)

b）关于访问的资料(访问目的、抵达和离开日期、要访问的地点、申请人与受邀个人的关系、资金来源)

c）邀请个人的信息(姓名、联系电话、地址、签名等)

（2）被邀请人的中国身份证、外国护照和永久居留证复印件。

R- 签证

申请人应当按照有关规定提交相关证明，并符合中国政府主管机关的有关要求。

S1- 签证

（1）受邀个人(在中国境内工作或者留学的外国人)的邀请函，其中包括：

a）申请人的资料(全名、性别、出生日期等)

b）访问情况(访问目的、抵达和离开日期、预定居住地、申请人与受邀个人之间的关系、资金来源)

c）邀请个人的信息(姓名、联系电话、地址、签名等)

（2）被邀请人的护照和居留证的复印件。

（3）证明申请人与受邀人士之间直系亲属关系的原件和复印件(结婚证、出生证明、公安局出具的亲属证明或者亲属关系公证)。

"直系亲属"是指18岁以下的配偶、父母、子女和岳父母。

我们谨提醒您：

S1签证持有人应当自入境之日起30日内向县级以上地方人民政府公安机关出入境管理部门或者在拟议的外国人居住证居住地提出申请。

S2- 签证

如探视家人的时间较短，请提供下列文件：

（1）受邀人(在中国境内工作、留学的外国人)发出的邀请函，其中包括：

a）申请人的资料(全名、性别、出生日期等)

b）关于访问的资料(访问目的、抵达和离开日期、访问地点、申请人与邀请人之间的关系、资金来源等)

c）邀请个人的信息(姓名、联系电话、地址、签名等)

（2）受邀个人(在中国工作、留学的外国人)的护照、居留证复印件。

（3）证明文件(结婚证、出生证明或者亲属公证)复印件，或其他证明申请人与受邀人之间家庭关系的证件。

"家庭成员"是指配偶、父母、儿子、女儿、子女的配偶、兄弟姐妹、祖父母、孙子、孙女和岳父母。

对于私人事务，应根据领事官员的要求提供文件，说明私人事务的性质。

X1- 签证

（1）中国学校或者其他单位出具的录取通知书原件和复印件。

（2）"中国留学签证申请书"(JW 201或JW 202)正本及复印件。

我们谨提醒您：

X1签证持有人应当自入境之日起30日内向县级以上地方人民政府公安机关办理出入境手续。

X2- 签证

中国学校或其他单位出具的录取通知书正本及复印件。

Z- 签证

下列文件之一：

（1）由中国政府人力资源和社会保障主管部门颁发的"中华人民共和国外国人就业许可证"和经中国有关单位正式批准出具的外国人就业邀请函或确认函。

（2）国家外国专家局颁发的在中国工作的外国专家许可证以及经正式授权的单位的邀请函或者REL发出的确认邀请函。

（3）由中国工商行政管理部门出具的外国企业常驻代表办事处的登记证明，以及中国有关单位发出的正式授权单位邀请函或确认函。

（4）由中国政府文化事务主管部门出具的商业演出批准文件或者经正式授权的单位的邀请函或者邀请函。

（5）由中国海洋石油总公司向外国人发出的海上石油作业邀请函；

我们谨提醒您：

持有Z签证的，应当自入境之日起30日内向县级以上地方人民政府公安机关申请出入境管理。

特别提醒：

（1）邀请信可采用传真、影印本或电脑打印的形式，但领事官员可要求申请人提交邀请信的原件。

（2）如有需要，领事人员可要求申请人提供其他证明文件或补充材料，或要求与申请人面谈。

（3）领事官员将根据申请人的具体情况决定是否签发签证，以及签证的有效期、逗留期限和入境次数。

（4）欲知详情，请浏览有关中国大使馆或总领事馆的网站。

Part V Discussion

1. What did you learn from this unit?
2. Talk about the process of applying Chinese Visa.

Part VI Writing

If you are a staff of a travel agency in Chengdu, now, there is foreign guest contact you want to consult the process, according to what you have learned in this unit, how can you help him? Try to make a dialogue.

Unit 4 | Tour Reservation

Learning objectives

1. Know the process about how to reserve the plane ticket and hotel.
2. Master the useful expressions in booking the plane ticket and hotel.

Part I Warming up

Match each airline company with their English name.

阿联酋航空	Air Berlin
中国国际航空	Delta Air Lines
卡塔尔航空	Emirates Airlines
汉莎航空	Lufthansa
柏林航空	Qatar Airways
中国东方航空	Air China
达美航空	United Airlines
美国联合航空	China Eastern Airlines

"I will prepare and some day my chance will come."
(我会做好准备，总有一天我的机会会到来。)

——Abraham Lincoln

Part II Reading

China International Airlines

China International Airlines Co., Ltd., abbreviated as "Air China", English name "Air China Limited", referred to as "Air China", its predecessor, China International Airlines was established in 1988. According to the Civil Aviation System Reform Plan approved by the State Council, in October 2002, China International Airlines, in conjunction with China Airlines Corporation and Southwest Airlines of China, established China Airlines Group, and set up a new China International Airlines basis on the air transport resources of the three parties. On September 30, 2004, it was supervised by the State-owned assets of the State Council. The Governor's Management Committee approved that Air China, as the central air transport company controlled by Air China Group, was formally established in Beijing. On December 15, 2004, China International Airlines Co., Ltd. was successfully listed in Hong Kong (stock code 0753) and London (trading code AIRC).

Air China's corporate logo is made up of "China International Airlines" and English "AIR CHINA". The symbol of Air China is Phoenix, and it is also the artistic deformation of English "VIP" (distinguished guests). The color is the red of Chinese tradition, with the moral of auspiciousness, perfection, harmony and happiness, and embodies the sincere feelings of Air China people serving the society and the eternal pursuit of safety cause.

Air China is the only civil aviation company carrying the national flag in China and a member of the Star Alliance, the world's largest aviation alliance. It has the first brand value of domestic airlines in the 2008 Beijing Olympic Games (the world brand laboratory rated 40.629 billion yuan in 2010). It is in a leading position in air passenger transport, freight and related services.

As of December 31, 2019, Air China (including its holding company) owns a total of 699 aircrafts of various types, mainly by Boeing and Airbus, with an average lifespan of 6.96 years. The company's passenger routes have expanded to 770, including 137 international, 27 regional and 606 domestic routes. The company flies to 43 countries (regions) and 187 cities, including 65 international, 3 regional, and 119 domestic cities. Through its collaboration with other Star Alliance member airlines, the company's route network has further extended to 1317 destinations in 195 countries.

After the reading please answer the questions below:
1. When was the China International Airline established?
2. How does the name of Air China come from?
3. What is the vision of the service of Air China?

Part III Listening

Listen to *dialogues* and finish the tasks.
Situational dialogue 1
Conversation: plane ticket reservation. The travel agency is making the plane ticket for the group of Chengdu.
Task: discussion

What does the dialogue talk about?

Mary: Good afternoon, this is ×× airline reservation line, what can I do for you?

Carol: Hello, I am Carol from Mingjiang travel agency, I'm calling to booking the tickets for our tour group.

Mary: Sure, we have three flights to Chengdu weekly: Monday, Wednesday, and Friday. The flights on Monday and Friday are direct and the one on Wednesday has a stopover in Shanghai. When were you thinking of flying to Chengdu?

Carol: Our group will depart at 17th of September, which is Friday.

Mary: Will this be round trip or one way?

Carol: Round trip returning the following Sunday.

Mary: How would you like to fly? Economy? Business? Or first class?

Carol: Business, please.

Mary: How many people are there in your group?

Carol: 22 in total.

Mary: OK, please give me a minute while I check price and availability. There are several seats still available. The flight will departs at 11:20 a.m. and arrives at Chengdu at 6:40 p.m. on local time.

Carol: Fine.

Mary: Let me confirm your information, one group with 22 people, 17th of September, is that right?

Carol: Yes, sure.

Mary: OK, please send me all the passengers' information, I'll complete the reservation.

Carol: I will send you later, thank you so much.

Mary: My pleasure, bye.

Situational dialogue 2

Context: The travel agency staff is helping his client to book the hotel.
Task: answer the questions below.
1. When will the client check-in?
2. How many people are there in the group?

Lily: Good afternoon, this is Jinjiang hotel, what can I do for you?

Carol: Hello, I am Carol from Mingjiang travel agency, I'm calling to booking the room for our tour group.

Lily: No problem, when will you check-in and how many people are there in your group?

Carol: 18th of September, 22 people in total for 3 nights.

Lily: OK, I need all the people's name and passport number.

Carol: I'll send you later.

Lily: OK, is there anything else I can help you?

Carol: No, Thank you very much.
Lily: My pleasure.

Situational dialogue 3
Context: Confirmation the travel information with the company in China.
Task: answer the questions below.
1. What are they talking about?
2. Why Eric make a call with the staff in the company in China?

Jack: Hello, this is Mingjiang travel agency in China, may I help you?
Carol: Hi, I'm Carol from the agency aboard, I'm calling to confirm the information of the tour group.
Jack: Sure.
Carol: They will arrive in Chengdu at 18th of September, and first sightseeing in Chengdu for 3 days, and then go to Dujiangyan to visit the Dujiangyan Irrigation System, and Mt. Qingcheng, and finally go to Jiuzhaigou, totally 9 days. So please contact the driver and tour guide to pick them up at the airport, the detail travel itinerary I'll send to your Email later, please check it.
Jack: Sure, keep in touch.
Carol: OK, good-bye.
Jack: Good-bye.

Part IV Vocabulary

Textbook	Word stress	Translation
referred	re-FERR-ed	参考；查阅
establish	es-TAB-lish	建立；创立
conjunction	con-JUNC-tion	结合；同时发生
deformation	de-for-MA-tion	变形
moral	MO-ral	道德的；精神上的
auspiciousness	aus-PI-cious-ness	吉兆
harmony	HAR-mony	协调；和睦
eternal	e-TER-nal	永恒的；不朽的
persuit	per-SUIT	追赶；追求
aviation	a-VIA-tion	航空；飞机制造业
alliance	a-LLIAN-ce	联盟；联合
brand	BRAND	品牌
domestic	do-MES-tic	国内的；家庭的
aircraft	AIR-craft	飞机
laboratory	la-BO-ra-tory	实验室

阅读译文

中国国际航空公司

中国国际航空有限公司，简称"国航"，英文名称"Air China"，前身是中国国际航空公司，成立于1988年。根据国务院批准的民航体制改革计划，2002年10月，中国国际航空公司与中华航空公司和西南航空公司联合成立了华航集团，并在三方航空运输资源的基础上成立了新的中国国际航空公司。在2004年9月30日，被总督管理委员会批准，国航作为航空集团控制的主要航空运输公司，总部设立于北京。2004年12月15日，中国国际航空公司在香港（股票代码0753)和伦敦（交易代码AIRC）成功上市。

国航公司标志由"中国国际航空公司"和英文"Air China"组成。中国国航的象征是凤凰，也是英文"贵宾"（贵宾）的艺术象征。红色是中国传统的红色，具有吉祥寓意。感悟、和谐、幸福，体现了国航为社会服务的真挚感情和对安全事业的永恒追求。

中国国航是中国唯一一家悬挂国旗的民航公司，也是世界上最大的航空联盟"星空联盟"的成员，拥有2008年北京奥运会国内航空公司第一品牌的价值（2010年世界品牌实验室评级406.29亿元）。该公司在航空客运、货运和相关服务方面处于领先地位。

截至2019年12月31日，国航（含控股公司）共拥有以波音、空中客车为主的各型飞机699架，平均机龄6.96年；经营客运航线已达770条，其中国际航线137条，地区航线27条，国内航线606条，通航国家（地区）43个，通航城市187个，其中国际65个，地区3个，国内119个；通过与星空联盟成员等航空公司的合作，将服务进一步拓展到195个国家（地区）的1317个目的地。

Part V Discussion

1. What did you learn from this unit?
2. What is the most important thing when you plan your trip?
3. Do you prefer a traditional hotel or other types of accommodations during the trip?

Part VI Writing

Your American friends Carol studying in Shanghai, China. He wants to travel to Chengdu during the winter break, and he is asking you to help him to reserve the plane ticket and the hotel in Chengdu. According to what you have learned in the unit, try to make a dialogue with your partner.

Unit 5 Tour Arrangement

 Learning objectives

1. Know the job of travel agency survey.
2. Master the process of the job of travel agency survey.

Part I Warming up

Please explain the main duties of a tour leader, local guide and scenic spots guide.

Suggested Answer: A tour leader leads a group overseas. His job entails ensuring the tourists get what the paid for, facilitating the flight, protecting the safety of tourists, solving problems and making sure they have a good time.

So, what do you think?

"A strong man will struggle with the storms of fate."
（一个坚强的人将与命运的风暴斗争。）

——Thomas Addison

Part II Reading

Southern provincial capital knows how to work and play

Giant pandas and a pleasant living environment are some of Chengdu's major attractions, but the capital of southwestern Sichuan province is also justifiably proud of its appeal to foreign investors.

By far, Chengdu boasts the presence of 212 Fortune 500 companies, including Intel, Texas Instruments and Dell, surpassing all other cities in China's central and western regions.

The provincial capital was chosen to host the upcoming 2013 Fortune Global Forum, making it the third city in the mainland to hold the significant business event after Shanghai and Beijing.

Chengdu's robust economic growth in recent years has attracted an increasing number of business travelers. Here are three attractions for business travelers.

1. Chengdu Giant Panda Breeding Research Base

The giant panda is the national treasure of China. There are fewer than 1,500 in the world, of which about 75 percent are found in Sichuan.

Located 10 kilometers away from downtown Chengdu, the Chengdu Panda Base has been recreated to follow pandas' natural habitats - large open grounds are built for the giant pandas to roam free, making it a great place to see the giant panda up close.

About 20 giant pandas live at the base. Other endangered species such as the red panda and the black-necked crane are also bred here.

2. Wide and narrow alleys

This tourist attraction is composed of three parallel alleys called Kuan Alley (Wide Alley), Zhai Alley (Narrow Alley) and Jing Alley (Well Alley).

The place is one of the top three historic, preserved areas in Chengdu. Most buildings are courtyards made of wood and bricks.

All three alleys are narrow lanes chock full of restaurants, and cafes as well as shops selling tea and curios.

3. Dujiangyan Irrigation System

The Dujiangyan Irrigation System, 58 km from Chengdu, which is the oldest existing irrigation project in the world, with a history of more than 2,000 years. It was designed to divert water without the use of dams and was built in 256 BC during the Warring States Period (475-221 BC).

Li Bing, an official of Sichuan at that time, was assigned to build an irrigation system on the Minjiang River with his son to prevent flooding. After they came up with the system, the Chengdu Plain was free of floods. Even today, the irrigation infrastructure still diverts the waters of the Minjiang River and distributes it efficiently to the fertile farmlands of the Chengdu Plain.

In 2000 the Dujiangyan Irrigation System was included in the list of UNESCO world heritage sites.

Sichuan is home to some of the spiciest - and many swear, tastiest - Chinese food. As the capital of Sichuan, Chengdu is obviously the place to try out authentic Sichuan cuisine. Hotpot in Chengdu should not be missed. Countless hotpot shops are operating throughout the city.

The famous Grandma Chen's Beancurd Restaurant serves Mapo tofu, one of the most popular dishes of Sichuan. Soft bean curd is served up with a fiery meat sauce. Another place worth trying is Long Chao Shou Special Restaurant, with its chain stores scattered throughout the city.

Zongfu Road, Chunxi Road and Jinli Street are the snack havens of Chengdu.

Several bar streets offer the chance to sample the authentic nightlife, including Jinli Street, South Renmin Road and Yulin district. Visitors can chit chat or play mahjong at local teahouses to help immerse themselves in famous local pastimes.

After the reading please answer the questions below:

1. Why has Chengdu attracted more and more tourists in recent years?
2. What can the tourists find in Chengdu?
3. What are the characteristics of the food in Chengdu?

Part III Listening

Listen to *dialogues* and finish the tasks.

Situational dialogue 1

Context: The travel agency staff is calling his client to confirm the trip information.

Task: answer the questions below.

1. Where will they go?
2. How long will they stay in Chengdu?
3. If you are a colleague at the airport, do you know how to help the client to check-in? Make a conversation with your partner.

Carol: (on the phone) Is that Eric?

Eric: Yes, I am.

Carol: This is Mingjiang travel agency, I'm calling you to confirm you trip information, you've booked a trip to Chengdu with us before.

Eric: Yes!

Carol: You've booked a trip to Chengdu for two people for nine days, and you have already paid, the price includes all the fees you don't need to pay anymore during the trip.

Eric: That all right.

Carol: OK, and you will start your trip on this Friday, so please make sure to take your passport and all your belongings to the airport in two hours advance, the departure time of your flight is 15:30 p.m., and one of my colleagues will wait for you at the airport to help you to Check-in.

Eric: Perfect, but how can we get in touch with her?

Carol: Wait a moment, I will send you her contact way, and the colleagues will pick you up at Chengdu Shuangliu international airport when you arrive.

Eric: Fine.

Carol: Your travel itinerary form I will send to your email, please check it as soon as possible, if you have any question, please contact me.

Eric: OK, thank you.

Carol: My pleasure, good bye.

Situational dialogue 2

Context: The travel agency staff is calling the guide in Chengdu to confirm the trip information.

Task: answer the questions below.
1. How can the guide find the guests at the airport?
2. When will the group arrive at Chengdu Shuangliu international airport?

Dally: Good morning, this is Dally's speaking.

Jack: Hi, Dally, this is Jack from Mingjiang travel agency.

Dally: Nice to hear your voice Jack.

Jack: I'm calling to confirm the information about the tour group in Chengdu.

Dally: Sure.

Jack: You have responsibilities for accompanying them during the whole trip, and they will arrive in Chengdu Shuangliu international airport at 6:00 a.m..

Dally: No problem, I'll arrive at the airport a half-hour before, and please send me the name list of guests and telephone number of the group leader, then I can get touch with them.

Jack: Sure, I'll send you later, and do you have the number of the driver?

Dally: Yes, I have.

Jack: OK, good. If you have any questions, please contact me.

Dally: Fine, Bye-bye.

Jack: Bye.

Part IV Vocabulary

Textbook	Word stress	Translation
province	PRO-vin-ce	省；领域
justifiably	JUST-ti-fi-ably	言之有理地
investor	in-VES-tor	投资人
appeal	a-PPEAL	吸引
giant	GIANT	巨大的
endangered	en-DAN-ger-ed	濒危的
crane	CRANE	吊车；起重机
alley	A-lley	小巷；小路
parallel	PA-ra-llel	平行线；对比
preserve	pre-SER-ve	保存；保护
lane	LANE	小巷；车道
Irrigation	ir-ri-GA-tion	灌溉
narrow	NA-rrow	狭窄的；有限的
dams	DAMS	海洋建筑的设计与分析
farmland	FARM-land	农田
authentic	au-THEN-tic	真正的；真实的
Spicy	SPI-cy	麻辣的
immerse	im-MER-se	沉浸；使陷入

阅读译文

南方省会的工作和玩耍

成都不仅有宜人的生活环境和大熊猫,它同样吸引着很多外国投资者。

到目前为止,成都拥有212家"财富500强"企业或分支机构,包括英特尔、德州仪器和戴尔,超过了中国中西部地区的其他城市。这座省会城市被选为2013年"财富"全球论坛的东道主,成为继上海和北京之后第三个举办大型商业活动的城市。成都近年来强劲的经济增长吸引了越来越多的商务旅客。这里有三个吸引商务旅客的景点。

1. 成都大熊猫繁殖研究基地

大熊猫是中国的国宝。世界上只有不到1500只,其中约75%在四川。成都熊猫基地位于距离成都市中心10公里的地方,为了跟随大熊猫的自然栖息习性,成都熊猫基地已经被重建——为大熊猫自在漫游建造了巨大的空地。这是一个近距离观察大熊猫的好地方。

大约有20只大熊猫生活在这个基地。其他濒危物种,如红熊猫和黑颈鹤也在这里繁殖生息。

2. 宽窄巷子

这个旅游景点由三条平行的小巷组成:宽巷(宽巷)、寨巷(窄巷)和井巷(井巷)。

这个地方是成都三大历史保护区之一。大多数建筑都是用木头和砖块砌成的。这三条小巷都是狭窄的小巷,挤满了餐馆、咖啡馆,还有卖茶和古玩的商店。

3. 都江堰灌溉系统

距成都市区58公里的都江堰灌溉系统是世界上现存最古老的灌溉工程,已有2000多年的历史。它的目的是不使用水坝来调水,建于公元前256年战国时期(公元前475年—公元前221年)。

李冰当时是四川的一名官员,他被指派与儿子一起在岷江上修建灌溉系统,以防止洪水泛滥。在他们提出这个系统之后,成都平原没有再遇洪灾。即使到了今天,灌溉基础设施仍然把岷江的水分流到成都平原肥沃的农田。

2000年,都江堰灌溉系统被列入联合国教科文组织世界遗产名录。

四川是盛产美食的地方。作为四川的省会,成都显然是品尝地道川菜的地方。成都的火锅不能错过。全市有无数的火锅店在营业。

著名的麻婆豆腐是四川最受欢迎的菜肴之一。软豆腐配上热辣的肉酱。另一个值得尝试的地方是龙抄手特色餐厅,其连锁店遍布全市。

总府路、春熙路、锦里街是成都的小吃天堂。数条酒吧街道提供了体验真实夜生活的机会,包括锦里街、人民南路和玉林区。游客可以在当地茶馆聊天或打麻将,参加当地著名的娱乐活动。

Part V Discussion

1. What did you learn from this unit?
2. Do you like travelling?
3. Talk with your partner about your most unforgettable travel experience.

Part VI Writing

Please design a one-day tour itinerary in Chengdu with your partner.

Module 3
Tour Guide Service

Unit 6 | Travel Introduction

 Learning objectives

1. Introduce a tour itinerary and its relevant service;
2. Get familiar with the tour reception plan;
3. Contact with the national guide in the destination;
4. Deal with different problems met by tourists before starting.

Part I Warming up

Task 1: Being a tour guide, you should know what to prepare before meeting the tourists for the first time. Make a discussion of what you should do.

Task 2: Decide whether the following statements are about an operator's responsibilities in a travel agency. Write T if it is, and F if it is not.

1. (   ) Make arrangements for transportation, hotel accommodation, car rental, etc.

2. (   ) Help clients make the best possible travel arrangements.

3. (   ) Provide information about customs regulations, required documents and currency exchange rates.

4. (   ) Prepare the guide badge, cash and the tour plan for the local tour guide.

5. (   ) Provide tourists with information about their destinations, such as the weather conditions and local customs.

6. (   ) Help tourists purchase foreign currency.

"Hard work beats talent when talent fails to work hard."
（当有天分的人不努力工作时，努力工作的人胜过有天分的人。）
——Kevin Durant

Part II Reading

Meeting for the First Time

We exchange greetings with people almost every day. Therefore, English for greetings is of primary importance in English oral practice. Good command of it can make you sound polite and sociable.

A greeting is a way of showing politeness and friendliness when we meet someone we know. Ways of greeting people vary from country to country. Chinese people often greet each other by asking, "Have you eaten?" or "Where are you going?" or even, "You are gaining weight!" But to Westerners, they may take it as an invitation, or they think that we are invading their privacy.

The usual formal greeting for the first time is a "How do you do?" with a firm handshake between men but a lighter touch between men and women. "How do you do?" is a greeting question, and the correct response is to repeat "How do you do?" You say this when shaking hands with someone.

"Good morning" or "Hello" is often said between nodding acquaintances; "How are you?" or "How is the family?" are expressed to someone you are familiar with and the most acceptable response for Chinese learners (also the most boring one) is "I am fine. Thank you, and you?"

Many Beginners use the expression "Nice to meet you" even when they meet with a person they have been introduced to before. This expression ("Nice to meet you") is used mostly at a first meeting, not after that. Instead, the person could say, "Nice to see you again".

After reading, please answer the questions below:
1. How do you greet people?
2. What would you like to say when you are introduced to another person?
3. What do you often say when you meet a person for the first time?

Part III Listening

Listen to *dialogues* and finish the tasks.
Situational dialogue 1
Context: Sherry Li, a tour guide, is speaking to Eric, the head of an American tour group on the phone.
Task: answer the questions below.
1. According to the dialogue, what does an average tourist want to know most about China?
2. Why do most tourists want to see more historical sites rather than artificial spots?

Eric: Hello!
Sherry Li: Hello, Eric. It's nice to hear your voice again.

Eric: Me too. I am glad to have received your itinerary so soon.

Sherry Li: I wonder what you and the group think of it. Do you have any suggestions?

Eric: Not at all. Actually, the whole group can't wait to see China.

Sherry Li: What do they want to know about China?

Eric: A lot of things, such as social situation, religion, culture, food and martial art.

Sherry Li: Well. So many things.

Eric: By the way, my friends want to visit more historical sites, but fewer artificial spots.

Sherry Li: OK. I will arrange more time for what you like.

Eric: Could we travel by train at least once?

Sherry Li: Certainly, at least we can go to Dujiangyan from Chengdu by train.

Eric: That's very good! Please tell me in advance if anything is changed.

Sherry Li: No problem! We will look forward to meeting you in China soon.

Situational dialogue 2

Context: Eric is meeting the tourists. They are talking about the weather.

Task: answer the questions below.

1. Has the tourist ever paid a visit to Southwest China before?
2. Did the weatherman make a correct prediction?
3. What is it like in autumn according to the dialogue?
4. Why does Eric think of autumn as a harvest season?
5. What does the tourist suggest during the stay in Chengdu?

Tourist: It's the first time that I have been to Southwest China.

Eric: Welcome! I hope you will have a good time.

Tourist: A nice day, isn't it?

Eric: Yes, it's good to see the sun, but it's quite different from the weather forecast.

Tourist: What did the weather forecast say?

Eric: It said it would be cloudy all day.

Tourist: I hope it will stay fine.

Eric: But autumn is coming, so it's getting colder soon.

Tourist: Yes, but I like this season because there are different kinds of scenery to enjoy.

Eric: The trees turn yellow or red and the mountains are decorated with colorful cloths.

Tourist: Great!

Eric: And we regard autumn as the harvest season. All fruits and crops ripe and are waiting to be harvested then.

Tourist: I wish I had a chance to pick them up and taste the fresh fruits.

Eric: Really?

Tourist: Why not spend some time doing it?

Eric: Let me see (look at the itinerary). If we have some free time in Chengdu, I can arrange it if you want me to.

Tourist: That's great. I will look forward to it.

Situational dialogue 3

Context: Now a tourist is late.

Task: discussion.

How would you handle this situation?

Tourist: Sorry to be late. I was caught up in a traffic jam. Am I the last one to arrive?
Eric: Yes, but it is okay.
Tourist: So sorry, I don't mean to be.
Eric: That's all right.
Tourist: Thanks for your kindness.
Eric: You are welcome.

Situational dialogue 4

Context: Eric, the tour leader is introducing the itinerary and requirements to the tourists.

Task: answer the questions below.
1. Where are the tourists from?
2. Before introducing the itinerary, what does Eric do?
3. How long will the tourists stay in Sichuan?
4. What places of interest will the tourists see in Dujiangyan?
5. What special instructions does Eric make to the tourists?

Eric: Good morning, dear friends! It's a great pleasure to share this China trip with you.
Tourist: Good morning, sir!
Eric: First of all, I would like to introduce myself. I am the leader of our trip. My name is Eric.
Tourist: Nice to meet you.
Eric: Let's count all the people.
Tourist: OK. Can we go?
Eric: Yes, everybody is here.
Tourist: Shall we go now?
Eric: Just a minute. From today on, I will take charge of all aspects of your food, shelter and travel. If you encounter any difficulties in the journey, you can come to me. I will try my best to help you coordinate and solve them. Of course, if there is anything I did not think of, I also welcome your valuable advice. I will correct it as soon as possible.
Tourist: Thank you!
Eric: Here is the brief introduction to your itinerary.
Day 1-2: Chengdu (Arrive in Chengdu by flight from New York.);
Day 3: Chengdu (One day trip in Chengdu including the visit of Du Fu Thatched Cottage, River-viewing Tower Park);
Day 4: Chengdu-Dujiangyan (Departure from Chengdu to Qingcheng Mountain after breakfast; Visit Dujiangyan including Dujiangyan Irrigation System, Qingcheng Mountain);
Day 5: Dujiangyan-Wenchuan (Depart from Dujiangyan to Wenchuan by coach. After

visiting Wenchuan earthquake ruins, go to Jiuzhaigou National Park;
Day 6-7: Visit Jiuzhaigou National Park;
Day8: After visiting Mianyang city, fly to Shanghai.

Tourist: A wonderful trip!
Eric: Please follow the local customs when you are in China.
Tourist: No Problem.
Eric: Our coach is outside.
Tourist: OK. Let's go.
Eric: Everyone, now please follow me.

Part Ⅳ Vocabulary

Textbook	Word stress	Translation
escort	E-scort	护送者；护卫队；受雇陪同某人
operator	O-pe-ra-tor	操作员；运营商；话务员；行家
accommodation	a-cco-mmo-DA-tion	住处；住宿；膳宿；和解；调解
custom	CUS-tom	惯例；风俗；海关；经常光顾
sociable	SO-cia-ble	好交际的；合群的；友好的
invade	in-VADE	侵略；侵犯；涌入；侵扰；干扰
acquaintance	a-CQUAIN-tance	熟人；认识；略有交情；了解
shelter	SHEL-ter	居所；庇护；遮蔽物；避难处；保护
coordinate	co-OR-di-nate	使协调；使相配合；搭配；坐标
itinerary	i-TI-ne-ra-ry	路线；旅行日程；旅程的；巡回的
martial	MAR-tial	战争的；军事的
artificial	ar-ti-FI-cial	人工的；假的；人为的；虚假的
historical	hi-STO-ri-cal	历史的；史学的；基于史实的

阅读译文

第一次见面

我们几乎每天都和人打招呼。因此，英语问候语在英语口语实践中具有重要意义。熟练掌握它能使你听起来更有礼貌和善于交际。

当我们遇到认识的人时，问候是一种表示礼貌和友好的方式。问候人们的方式因国家而异。中国人经常问对方："您吃了吗？"或者"您要去哪里？"甚至，"您最近长胖了点儿！"但是对于西方人来说，他们可能会把它当作邀请，或者他们认为我们侵犯了他们的隐私。

通常第一次正式的问候是"您好吗？"男人之间的握手很有力，但男人和女人之间的接触比较轻。"您好吗？"是一个问候问题，正确的回答是重复"您好吗？"当你和某人握手时，你会这么说。

> "早上好"或"您好"经常在点头的熟人之间说,"您好吗?"或者"家庭情况如何?"向你熟悉的人表达,中国学习者(也是最觉得单调的人)最能接受的回答是"我很好。谢谢,您呢?"
>
> 许多初学者使用"很高兴见到您",即使他们遇到了一个他们以前介绍过的人。这个表达("很高兴见到您")主要用于第一次见面,而不是之后。相反,那个人会说:"很高兴再次见到您"。

Part V Discussion

1. What did you learn from this unit?
2. Give a presentation to meet the tourists.
3. Suppose you are a tour leader; you have received a group of 22 travelers. How to introduce the itinerary to the tourists?

Part VI Writing

Task : Suppose you are an operator of a travel agency. You just received an enquiry email from Jim asking for some information about travel programs to Sichuan. Reply to the email based on the following information.

1. The best season to travel to Sichuan: from June to the beginning of October.
2. Famous scenic spots: Jiuzhaigou, Huanglong, Ermei Mountain, Leshan Giant Buddha statue.
3. Other recommendation: Most tourists highly praise the food in Sichuan. It's worth trying.
4. Recommended itinerary: It depends on people's particular requirements. There are several most favored itineraries attached for reference.

Unit 7 | Check in at the Airport

Learning objectives

1. Understand the airport signs;
2. Tell the regulations on free baggage allowance;
3. Check in the luggage;
4. Identify schedule information.

Part I | Warming up

Task 1: Match the following articles which are prohibited to be carried onto the plane with their corresponding pictures.

knife   gun   inflammable and explosive materials
toxic chemicals   endangered plant
1._____   2._____   3._____   4._____   5._____

Task 2: The following are some useful expressions for checking in at the airport. Do you know any other expressions for a tour guide and a tourist for checking in?

For a tour guide

1. I think we should start earlier. It may take some time on the way. There are always many traffic jams in this city.
2. You'll have to be at the airport something like an hour before the plane takes off to have some time to go through the check-in formalities and other things.
3. You'd better have your passport ready.
4. Do you have any seat preferences?
5. Do you need any pills/medicine for airsickness?

For a tourist

1. Could you explain the free baggage allowance to me?
2. Where do we check in our luggage?
3. When will the flight begin boarding?
4. Could you please tell me where the International Departure is?
5. Is this the counter for checking in of the Flight MH235 to Kuala Lumpur, please?

_____
_____
_____
_____
_____
_____
_____

"Whatever makes you different is what makes you stronger."
（那些让你更加强大的因素也是使你与众不同的因素。）

——Eva Chen

Part II Reading

Chengdu Shuangliu International Airport

Chengdu Shuangliu International Airport, located in Chengdu, Sichuan Province, western China, is the fourth largest aviation hub in the mainland of China. It is also an international aviation hub being actively built in Western China to connect the world.

In 2018, the passenger throughout of Chengdu Shuangliu International Airport reached

52.95 million. At present, Ethiopian Airlines, United Airlines, Royal Dutch Airlines, All Nippon Airlines, Qatar Airlines, China International Airlines, Sichuan Airlines and other Chinese and foreign airlines operate here. As of May 31, 2020, there are 363 routes at Chengdu Airport, including 128 international (regional) routes, 217 domestic routes, 18 international routes through domestic stops.

Chengdu Shuangliu International Airport has direct flights to San Francisco, Los Angeles, New York, Amsterdam, Frankfurt, Moscow, Paris, Prague, Madrid, London, St. Petersburg, Copenhagen, Melbourne, Sydney, Auckland, Oceania, Addis Ababa, Mauritius and major cities in Asia.

Chengdu Shuangliu International Airport is committed to providing high-level operation platform for global airlines. Two terminal buildings with an area of 500, 000 square meters. Two runways for taking off and landing of A380 aircraft.

Chengdu Shuangliu International Airport provides high standard services for flights and passengers from all over the world. Provide bonded aviation fuel for international flights, exempt 144-hour transit for foreign passengers, and provide 7 × 24-hour customs clearance guarantee for all international flights, international passengers and import and export goods.

Chengdu Shuangliu International Airport is speeding up the construction of an "interconnected, globally radiated" international aviation hub in Western China, and constantly improving the route network to Europe, the United States, Africa, Asia and Oceania.

After reading, please answer the questions below:

1. Is Chengdu Shuangliu International Airport largest aviation hub in the mainland of China?

2. How many routes are there in Chengdu Shuangliu International Airport?

3. How do you prove that "Chengdu Shuangliu International Airport is one of the largest aviation hubs in the mainland of China"?

Part III Listening

Listen to *dialogues* and finish the tasks.

Situational dialogue 1

Context: The tour leader Eric goes to a clerk of the airline for help.

Task: answer the questions below.

1. What does MH235 mean?
2. When will the flight depart?
3. Try to rehearsal this dialogue.

Eric: Excuse me. We are to transfer to Flight MH235 to Kuala Lumpur. Can you help me?

Clerk: Yes. May I have your tickets?

Eric: Here are 22 tickets for seven families. Can we have our seats as close to each other as possible? Or can a family have their seats together at least? You know kids should be taken care of by their parents.

Clerk: I'll try my best, but I cannot promise anything because this is a connecting flight and the aircraft is quite full now. I can only give you available seats.

Eric: OK. It's accepted.

Clerk: Here are you tickets and boarding pass. I have given you seats as close together as possible. The departure time is 09:55, Gate E3.

Eric: Could you tell me the way to Departure Gate E3?

Clerk: Take the escalator down to the next floor, get on the travellator to the departure area, and then you will easily find Gate E3. You may wait in the departure lounge for boarding as there is not much time left.

Eric: Thank you.

Clerk: Not at all. Goodbye.

Eric: Bye.

Situational dialogue 2

Context: The tour leader Eric is checking in for the tour member.

Tasks: answer the questions below.

1. What does OD522 mean?
2. What does the tour leader Eric show to the clerk?
3. Summarize the procedures of check-in at the airport.

Eric: Hello, we are a group of 22 people going to Chengdu by OD522.

Clerk: May I see your tickets and passports, please?

Eric: Sure, here you are.

Clerk: How many pieces of luggage would you like to check in?

Eric: Thirty pieces altogether.

Clerk: Here are your tickets, passports and boarding pass. Your luggage claim tags are attached to the tickets cover.

Eric: Thank you.

Clerk: You're welcome.

Situational dialogue 3

Context: The tour leader Eric is checking baggage in.

Task: answer the questions below.

1. What kind of seats would the tour leader like?
2. Is the luggage overweight?
3. What does free baggage allowance mean?
4. What does the leader show to the clerk?
5. Summarize the procedures of checking baggage in.

Eric: Excuse me. Should I check in here for taking Flight OD522 to Chengdu?

Clerk: Yes, sir. May I have your passport and flight tickets, please?

Eric: Sure, here are 22 tickets and passports. We are from the same tour group. Can we have 10 window and 12 aisle seats.

Clerk: Let me see. OK. No problem. Do you have any pieces of luggage to check in?

Eric: Yes. We have 28 suitcases and two bags.

Clerk: Would you please put them on the scale?

Eric: Of course. They are not overweight, are they?

Clerk: I'm sorry. They are 5kg over.

Eric: That's too bad. It must be because of the brochures.

Clerk: I see you don't have any carry-on luggage. Probably you could pick some brochures out of your luggage and take them with you.

Eric: Good idea. Could you explain the free baggage allowance to me?

Clerk: Of course. On continental flights to Chengdu, your free baggage allowance is not more than 25kg each.

Eric: I see.

Clerk: Alright, here are your baggage claim tags, right tickets, boarding passes and passports.

Eric: When is the boarding time?

Clerk: The boarding time is 8:45 p.m. and you will board from Gate 18.

Eric: How can I find Gate 18 from here?

Clerk: Take the escalator over there and turn left. You'll see the sign.

Eric: Thank you very much.

Part IV Vocabulary

Textbook	Word stress	Translation
regulation	re-gu-LA-tion	管理；规则；规定的；平常的
allowance	a-LLOW-ance	津贴；补贴；补助；限额；免税额
schedule	SCHE-dule	计划（表）；时间表；一览表
prohibit	pro-HI-bit	禁止；阻止；使不可能
inflammable	in-FLAM-ma-ble	易燃的；易激动的；易激怒的
explosive	ex-PLO-sive	易爆炸的；易爆发的；可能引起冲动的
toxic	TO-xic	有毒的；引起中毒的
preference	PRE-fe-rence	偏爱；爱好；喜爱；最喜爱的东西
board	BOARD	董事会；木板；膳食；上（飞机、车等）
aviation	a-vi-A-tion	航空；飞行术；飞机制造业
hub	HUB	中心；毂；木片
domestic	do-MES-tic	国内的；家庭的；驯养的；国货；佣人

Textbook	Word stress	Translation
commit	co-MMIT	犯罪；把…交托给；使…承担义务
terminal	TER-mi-nal	航空站；终点站；终端机；末端
exempt	e-XEMPT	免除；获豁免；豁免
radiate	RA-di-ate	流露；辐射；发散；向周围伸展
available	a-VAI-la-ble	可获得的；可购得的；可找到的；有空的
escalator	ES-ca-la-or	自动扶梯；电动楼梯；滚梯
travelator	TRA-ve-la-tor	移动走道；自动人行道（等于travolater）
claim	CLAIM	要求；声称；需要；认领；索赔；断言
brochure	bro-CHURE	资料手册

阅读译文

成都双流国际机场

成都双流国际机场位于中国西部四川省成都市，是中国大陆第四大航空枢纽。它也是一个"活跃"在中国西部的连接世界的国际航空枢纽。

2018年，成都双流国际机场旅客达5295万人次。目前，埃塞俄比亚航空公司、联合航空公司、荷兰皇家航空公司、全日空航空公司、卡塔尔航空公司、中国国际航空公司、四川航空公司等中外航空公司均在这里运营。截至2020年5月31日，成都机场共有363条航线，其中国际（地区）128条，国内217条，经停国内转国际18条。

成都双流国际机场有直飞旧金山、洛杉矶、纽约、阿姆斯特丹、法兰克福、莫斯科、巴黎、布拉格、马德里、伦敦、圣彼得堡、哥本哈根、墨尔本、悉尼、奥克兰、大洋洲、亚的斯亚贝巴、毛里求斯和亚洲主要城市的航班。

成都双流国际机场致力于为全球航空公司提供高水平的运营平台。两栋航站楼，面积达50万平方米。有两条供A380飞机起飞和降落的跑道。

成都双流国际机场为来自世界各地的航班和旅客提供高标准的服务。为国际航班提供保税航空燃料，为外国旅客免除144小时过境，为所有国际航班、国际旅客和进出口货物提供7×24小时的通关担保。

成都双流国际机场正在加快建设西部"互联、辐射全球"的国际航空枢纽，不断完善通往欧洲、美国、非洲、亚洲和大洋洲的航线网络。

Part V Discussion

1. Research online for information about famous airports in the world.
2. Suppose you are a tour leader; you have received a group of 22 travelers. How to help

them check-in at the airport?

Part VI Writing

Task: Fill in the Arrival Card according to the given information.

Li Ying, an English teacher, was born in Chengdu on July 8th, 1982. She takes Flight HU7915 from Chengdu to New York to attend a meeting and stay at Hilton Hotel in New York. Her passport number is E09800988, and her mobile phone number is 136×××× 0736. You can also contact her through the email to Liy_Rose@hotmail.com.

USA PASSENGER ARRIVAL CARD

Flight number_____
Overseas port where you board THIS aircraft_____
Passport number_____
Nationality as shown on passport_____
Family name_____
Given or first name_____
Date of birthday _____ month_____ year_____
Country of birth_____
Occupation or job_____
Full contact or residential address in New York_____
Email_____
Mobile/phone number_____

Unit 8 | National Guide

Learning objectives

1. Introduce a tour itinerary and its relevant service;
2. Get familiar with the tour reception plan;
3. Contact with the national guide in the destination.

Part I Warming up

Task 1: Being a tour guide, you should be familiar with the logos of different travel agencies. Match each logo with its agency's English name.

A._____

B._____

C._____

D._____

1. China Travel Service
2. China International Travel
3. China Comfort Travel
4. China Youth Travel Service

Task 2: Please explain the main duties of a tour leader, local guide and scenic spots guide.

Tour leader	
Local guide	
Scenic spots guide	

"Once you replace negative thoughts with positive ones, you'll start having positive results."

（一旦你用积极的想法代替消极的想法，你就会开始获得积极的结果。）

——Willie Nelson

Part II   Reading

On the Way to the Hotel

Ladies and gentlemen, welcome to China. My name is Victor Zhang, and I'm your guide here in Chengdu. This is Mr Wang, our driver. We'll be using this bus for the next few days. If you have any requests, please do let me know. I sincerely hope that you will enjoy your stay here.

Now, we are on our way to your hotel, the famous Jingjiang Hotel. It will take us about 30 minutes to get there. The time here in Chengdu now is 17:10. We are 13 hours ahead of New York, so you need to move your watches on by 13 hours if you haven't done so yet.

Coming out of the airport and driving all the way, we have now entered the city of Chengdu. As we mentioned earlier, the city of Chengdu has its location and name more than 2300 years of history, and in this 2300 years have never been relocated, changed the city name. However, this does not prevent Chengdu from having its own politics in different historical periods.

There are many nicknames with economic and cultural characteristics. During the Warring States Period, Qin annexed Shu. The city of Chengdu became the King of Shu, the Prime Minister of Shu and the Shu under the control of the Qin Central Government. At that time, the capital of the Qin Dynasty was Xianyang, so after the reconstruction, Chengdu had a nickname, Qin Cheng. Because Chengdu is located in the plain, it is easy to attack in the era of war disputes. It is difficult to defend the disadvantageous position. Therefore, after the completion of the city construction, the construction of the city wall began. It is an extension of the Great Wall.

The legendary tortoise has contributed a lot to the construction of the city wall, so Chengdu has another name "tortoise city". However, the subsequent political and economic developments reflected the limitations of Qin Cheng. It only considers Chengdu's political and cultural centrality but neglects its long-term position. The economic center position formed in the period with geographical advantages. The Qin government had to build a new economic center in the southwest of Qin Cheng (actually a market for agriculture, trade, industry and commerce field). The new city was built in obscurity, because it was adjacent to Qin Cheng. Relatively speaking, it is small in both scope and scale, so it is called a small town. Nevertheless, there were no small characters in Qin Dynasty. It was meant to be called "less", so the new city was named Chengdu Shaocheng. We will stay and go sightseeing in Chengdu for three days.

Well, now we arrive at the hotel. Please remember to bring all your belongings.

After reading, please answer the questions below:

1. If the time in Chengdu now is 17:10, what is the time in New York?
2. How does Chengdu get the nickname "Qin Cheng"?
3. Why is Chengdu also called Shaocheng?

Part III Listening

Listen to *dialogues* and finish the tasks.

Situational dialogue 1

Context: The tour guide Sherry Li is making a welcome speech to the tourists.

Task: answer the questions below.

1. What is "King Long" in the dialogue?
2. In western culture does the dragon enjoy a good reputation.
3. What does the dragon symbolize in China?
4. What is the special meaning of the color "golden" in Chinese culture?

Sherry Li: Good evening, ladies and gentlemen. Welcome to Chengdu.
Tourist: Thank you. May I ask you a question?
Sherry Li: Sure.
Tourist: The brand of this nice coach is "King Long". What is the meaning?
Sherry Li: I believe it means "the Golden Dragon".
Tourist: In the West, the dragon has an different meaning, and sometimes it is also depicted as a devil or demon. What does it symbolize in China?
Sherry Li: Well, in ancient China, the dragon, was a symbol of the emperors, was a kind and mysterious animal that can fly very fast and spout water.
Tourist: Really Then it seems that we are like emperors now.
Sherry Li: And the ladies are like queens. (laughter)
Tourist: You're so humorous! What's the special meaning of "golden" in this mark then?
Sherry Li: The color gold was the symbol, which was also the favorite color of the emperors.
Tourist: It's so interesting.

Sherry Li: The golden dragon will give you a pleasant trip to China. Let's drive it now.

Situational dialogue 2

Context: Tour guide Sherry Li is answering the tourist David's questions in Chengdu.

Tasks: answer the questions below.
1. Where will the tourists get their baggage?
2. Does Sherry Li work only work in their spare time?
3. Are the tourist's natives or foreigners? How do you get it?

Sherry Li: Good afternoon, ladies and gentlemen. Welcome to Chengdu.

Tourist: Thank you. But excuse me, where is my baggage?

Sherry Li: Don't worry about it. Your baggage will be sent to the hotel on another bus.

Tourist: Thanks a lot. May I have your name, please?

Sherry Li: My name is Sherry.

Tourist: Are you a part-time guide?

Sherry Li: No, I'm a full-time one. I'm from China International Travel Service, Chengdu Branch.

Tourist: Which hotel shall we stay?

Sherry Li: The Jingjiang Hotel. It is a luxurious five-star hotel.

Tourist: What is the bus number?

Sherry Li: It is 84176. Please do not forget it.

Tourist: By the way, what's the local time now?

Sherry Li: It's 6:15 p.m. Beijing time.

Situational dialogue 3

Context: Tour guide Sherry Li and tourist David are talking about the city.

Task: answer the questions below.
1. Is Chengdu famous for its mountains?
2. Was Dujiangyan Irrigation System completed in 306?
3. What is the Dujiangyan Irrigation System known?
4. How did the Chengdu Plain become one of the most fertile places in China?

Sherry Li: Welcome to Chengdu. I hope you will like it here.

David: It looks great here, especially the far-off mountains.

Sherry Li: Indeed, but Chengdu is not only well-known for its mountains.

David: Really? What is Chengdu famous for then?

Sherry Li: It is a famous Chinese historical and cultural city. Chengdu enjoys a world reputation for Dujiangyan Irrigation System.

David: I see. When was it built?

Sherry Li: It was built in Qin dynasty by the local people under the guidance of Li Bing and his son.

David: What is it like?

Sherry Li: It's one of the world's first irrigation system. It consists of three main parts: the Fish Mouth Water-Dividing Dam, the Flying Sand Fence and the Bottle-Neck Channel.

David: Sounds interesting.

Sherry Li: When the construction was completed, the dam system automatically diverted the Minjiang River and channeled it into irrigation canals. Gradually, the Chengdu Plain turned into one of the most fertile places in China. Since 1949, expansion has been undertaken, and at present, the system works very effectively. It irrigates farming land across 33 counties in West Sichuan Province. The system benefits local people, and the people are proud of the system.

David: Terrific!

Situational dialogue 4

Context: Tour guide Sherry Li and tour leader Eric are talking about a travel arrangement.

Task: answer the questions below.

1. Does Sherry Li want to change the itinerary?
2. What is Sherry Li's schedule on the fourth day?
3. What is Mt. Qingcheng famous for?
4. From where will Eric leave for Shanghai?

Sherry Li: Good morning, Eric.

Eric: Good morning, Miss Li. Come in, please!

Sherry Li: I hope we can spend a couple of minutes talking about the itinerary.

Eric: Fine. Please take a seat. Would you like some tea?

Sherry Li: O.K. Thanks.

Eric: Well, I received from your travel service before we started. I hope there is nothing to change.

Sherry Li: No, I have just gone over the itinerary again with you.

Eric: That's fine.

Sherry Li: First we will stay and go sightseeing in Chengdu for 3 days and then go to Dujiangyan to visit the Dujiangyan Irrigation System. The next destination is Mt. Qingcheng.

Eric: That's one of the birthplaces of Daoism, right?

Sherry Li: Yes. After that you will take a bus to Wenchuan where you will stay for one day. Then there will be another two days left for you to visit Jiuzhaigou National Park, including going to the beautiful city of Mianyang, in which you'll fly to Shanghai.

Eric: Is that the last spot?

Sherry Li: Yes, and we will stay for another two days.

Eric: Perfect! Thank you very much for the arrangement.

Sherry Li: My pleasure. If there is anything else, I can do. Please let me know.
Eric: Sure.
Sherry Li: See you.

Situational dialogue 5
Context: Sherry Li, the tour guide is talking about meal arrangements with the tour leader Eric.

Task: answer the questions below.
1. What is the breakfast like according to the arrangement?
2. Why does Eric think it's unnecessary to have lunch in a Chinese restaurant?
3. What will the group have for lunch?
4. According to the arrangement, will supper be provided?

Eric: Miss Li, what are the meal arrangements for the tour group tomorrow?
Sherry Li: Well, we'll have breakfast at 7 o'clock on the third floor of the hotel. It is a buffet style with many options.
Eric: OK. How about lunch?
Sherry Li: After the morning visit, we'll have lunch in a Chinese restaurant.
Eric: Mm... we do like Chinese food, but what about lunch in a Western restaurant for a change?
Sherry Li: Are you sure you wouldn't like to have a full Chinese meal?
Eric: No, that's not necessary. We need to have an early lunch tomorrow as we will be leaving at 2:00 pm for the airport. I think the group would appreciate being able to have just a sandwich for lunch.
Sherry Li: Oh, I see. I know a Western café nearby. Shall we go there?
Eric: Is it far from the scenic spot?
Sherry Li: No. It'll take only about ten minutes to get there.
Eric: That's fine. Thank you.

Part IV Vocabulary

Textbook	Word stress	Translation
sincerely	sin-CERE-ly	真诚地；诚实地
characteristic	cha-rac-te-RIS-tic	典型的；特征；特性；特色
annex	an-NEX	强占，并吞
nickname	NICK-NAME	绰号；昵称；给…取绰号
extension	ex-TEN-sion	延长；延期；扩大；伸展
legendary	LE-gen-da-ry	传说的，传奇的
subsequent	SUB-se-quent	后来的，随后的
centrality	cen-TRA-li-ty	中心地位，向心性，接近

Textbook	Word stress	Translation
commerce	COM-merce	贸易；商业；商务
obscurity	ob-SCU-ri-ty	无名；费解；晦涩；昏暗
adjacent	a-DJA-cent	邻近的，毗连的
brand	BRAND	铭记；印…商标于；商标；烙印
depict	de-PICT	描绘；描画；描写；描述；刻画
symbolize	SYM-bo-lize	象征；是…的象征；代表
spout	SPOUT	嘴；水柱；喷水；滔滔不绝地说
luxurious	lu-XU-rious	奢侈的；丰富的；特级的
irrigation	i-rri-GA-tion	灌溉；水利；冲洗
divert	di-VERT	使转向；使绕道；使分心
fertile	FER-tile	肥沃的；能产生好结果的
variety	va-RIE-ty	多样；种类；杂耍；多样化

阅读译文

在去酒店的路上

女士们先生们，欢迎来到中国。我叫张维克多，是您在成都的导游。这是王先生，我们的司机。接下来的几天我们要用这辆车。如果您有任何要求，请告诉我。我真诚地希望您在这里过得愉快。

现在，我们正在去往您们的饭店，也就是著名的锦江宾馆的路上。到那里大约需要30分钟。现在成都的时间是17:10。我们比纽约早13个小时，所以如果您还没有把手表往前拨的话，您需要把它往前拨13个小时。

从机场出来，我们现在已经进入了成都。成都这座历史文化名城是迄今为止唯一一座拥有2300余年历史、城址不迁、城名不易的古城。而这并不妨碍成都在不同的历史时期形成自己的政治格局。

这里有许多具有经济和文化特征的称号。战国时期，秦兼并蜀地。成都成为蜀王、蜀相、秦中央政权统辖管理下的治所。当时，秦朝的都城是咸阳，所以重建后，成都有了一个称谓——秦城。由于成都地处平原，在战乱时期很容易受到攻击。不利地位对于防御而言是困难的。因此，在城市建设完成后，城墙开始修建。它是长城的延伸。

传说中乌龟为城墙的修建做出了巨大的贡献，所以成都有了另一个名字"龟城"。然而，随后的政治经济发展也反映出秦城的局限性。它只考虑成都的政治文化中心地位，而忽略了成都的长期地位。经济中心地位形成于具有地域优势的时期。秦国政府不得不在秦城西南部建立一个新的经济中心（实际上是一个农业、贸易、工商业市场）。这座新城市因毗邻秦城而默默无闻。相对而言，它的范围和规模都很小，所以被称为"小城"。但秦朝尚无小字。这座城市本来打算被称为"少"，后被命名为"成都少城"。我们将在成都停留观光3天。

好了，现在我们到酒店了。请记得带上您所有东西。

Part V Discussion

1. What did you learn from this unit?
2. Suppose you are a tour guide, how do you introduce a city in brief?
3. How does a tour guide cooperate with the tour leader?

Part VI Writing

Task 1: Sum up the main steps of delivering a welcome speech on the way to the hotel by filling in the following blanks with reference to reading.

1. Introduce_____ and _____, and express good wish to the tourists;
2. Say something about_____;
3. Introduce the basic information of the_____;
4. Explain the scene along the way;
5. Brief on arrangements in the next few days.

Task 2: Suppose you are a tour guide of your hometown. Write a welcome speech to a tour group from abroad with reference to the steps in Task 1.

Unit 9 | Local Guide

Learning objectives

1. Learn about the famous scenic spots in Sichuan.
2. Introduce the famous scenic spots in Sichuan the tourists.
3. Make requests on behalf of the tourists.
4. Make a tour schedule.
5. Deal with different problems met by tourists during sightseeing.

Part I Warming up

Task 1: Discuss with your classmates about Chengdu. If you have been there, talk about your experience; if you haven't, tell the scenic spots you have heard of.

Task 2: Each of the following pictures shows a famous scenic spot in Chengdu. Match each picture with its English name.

1. Du Fu Thatched Cottage

2. Chengdu Wuhou Temple

3. Precious Light Monastery

4. Sangxingdui Museum

A.

B.

C.

D.

"Perfection is not attainable, but if we chase perfection we can catch excellence."
（完美是无法触及的，但是如果我们追求完美，就可以做到卓越。）

——Vince Lombardi

Part II Reading

Chengdu Wuhou Temple

Wuhou Temple was constructed in memory of Zhu Geliang, who was a well-known strategist and statesman during the Three Kingdoms Period.

China has a recorded history of some 3600 years. It began with the Shang Dynasty (16th-11th century BC). The whole ancient history is divided into three stages. The first stage is the primitive society. The history was much associated with the presumed pre-xia Dynasty 21st-16th century BC). The second major stage lasted from about 2000 to 200 BC.

The history dated the beginning of the slave society from the Xia Dynasty. The third stage extended from 221BC to the opium war of 1840. Historical doc names the third stage as the Feudal Imperial Society. At the end of the Eastern Han, the feudal society in China came into a period of disunity. Traditionally it is called the Three Kingdoms Period.

Towards the end of the Eastern Han, a great peasant rebellion broke out. Many local officials became autonomous regional warlords. They suppressed the rebellion, and at the same time they took the opportunity to build up their own political and military strength. Finally, the warlords carved the Han Empire into three kingdoms of Wei, Shu and Wu.

A classic Chinese novel is the Romance of the Three Kingdoms. The novel is so famous that most Chinese families each have a copy. The novel traces the rise and fall of the three kingdoms, and vividly depicts the turbulent social conditions at that time. Cao cao and his son established

as the Kingdom of Wei at Luoyang. Actually, Cao cao controlled North China homeland. The other two rivals soon proclaimed themselves emperors elsewhere. The Kingdom of Wu, with its capital at Nanjing occupied Changjiang Valley. The kingdom of Shu controlled Sichuan and parts of the Southwestern China highland. Its capital was in Chengdu.

Wuhou Temple is much associated with the Kingdom of Shu. It is a memorial to Zhu Geliang, Prime Minister of the kingdom. Wuxianghou was a top official title conferred upon Zhu Geliang when he serried the kingdom. After his death, another title was given to him. It was zhongwubou. People respectfully called him wuhou.

If you like travelling, then come and enjoy the party and the humane landscape. You'll be surprised at its exquisite architecture and rich history.

After reading, please answer the questions below:
1. How much do you know Zhu Geliang?
2. What kind of society was Shu Kingdom in?
3. What is the novel "the Romance of the Three Kingdoms" mainly about?
4. What titles did Zhu Geliang ever win?

Part III Listening

Listen to *dialogues* and finish the tasks.
Situational dialogue 1
Context: The local guide Gary Li meets Eric, the tour leader, in the lobby while waiting for the tourists.

Task: answer the questions below.
1. When will they visit the temple?
2. What is not allowed in the temple?
3. What should the tourists bring?
4. Try to rehearsal this dialogue.

Gary Li: Good morning, Eric.
Eric: Good morning, Mr Garry.
Gary Li: Did you sleep well last night?
Eric: Very well, thank you. May I have a look at the schedule, please?
Gary Li: Yes, here you are.
Eric: Ah, we'll visit the temple at 3:30 p.m.. I understand that people can't take photographs in Buddhist temples. Is that true?
Gary Li: Yes. According to local beliefs, the statues inside the temple should not be photographed, but you can take pictures outside the buildings.
Eric: All right. I'll tell the group when we get there.

Gary Li: Good. Also, I think we'd better remind everyone to bring umbrellas or raincoats with them because there is a rain forecast today.

Eric: OK. I'll tell everybody now.

Gary Li: So, we can all have breakfast and be ready to leave at 8:30 a.m., is that OK?

Eric: Yes, see you later.

Gary Li: See you.

Situational dialogue 2

Context: Gary Li is telling the tour group about the tour schedule for the day and answering some questions.

Tasks: answer the questions below.
1. Will the tourists visit the Du Fu Thatched Cottage at first?
2. Who was Du Fu?
3. Where will they visit next day?

Gary Li: Good morning. Now I'd like to introduce our schedule for today. First, we will go to Du Fu Thatched Cottage. It is a trendy place, and we have two hours there to enjoy all the sights. Next, we are going to pay a visit to River-viewing Tower Park. At 12 o'clock, we'll have lunch in a particular local restaurant, one of my favorites! Then in the afternoon, we are going to visit a Buddhist temple. Does anyone have any questions?

Tourist: Yeah, can you tell me who Du Fu was?

Gary Li: Du Fu was born in Gongxian 9-county, Henan Province in 712. He was also known as Du Zimei. He spent the greater part of his boyhood in Luoyang. In 746, he went to Chang'an, in an attempt to obtain an official post. However, he had only reached a minor post as he entered the age of fifty. In 759, he resigned and came to Chengdu. He died in 770.

Tourist: So, what's so special about the Thatched Cottage?

Gary Li: At present, it serves as a museum. It has a rich collection of over 30,000 bound volumes and 2,000 cultural relics beside Du Fu' poems, which have been translated into many languages.

Tourist: Can we stop somewhere to buy local handicrafts and souvenirs?

Gary Li: Yes, of course. There's a bazaar next to the Thatched Cottage. You can buy handicrafts there after visiting the temple this afternoon.

Tourist: Are we going to see any art museums?

Gary Li: Yes, sir. We'll visit the Chengdu Art Museum tomorrow. We don't have time today.

Tourist: Thank you very much.

Situational dialogue 3

Context: Gary Li is telling the tourists about the Du Fu Thatched Cottage and answering some questions.

Task: answer the questions below.
1. Whom was Du Fu Thatched Cottage in memory?
2. Who wrote Caotang on the board?
3. What does the couplet mean?

Gary Li: Well, here we are. This place is called Du Fu Thatched Cottage. As I said, it was constructed in memory of Du Fu.

Tourist: Wow, so wonderful! Can we take photos here?

Gary Li: Sure. You'll find it is very photogenic.

Tourist: So apart from being beautiful, why is it so famous? Can you tell us something about its history, please?

Gary Li: Of course! Now please look up at the horizontal board on the top of the entrance gate. Two big Chinese characters written on the board say: "Caotang". It means the Thatched Cottage. It was written a Prince of Qing Dynasty. A couplet hangs on either side of the entrance, which says, "The cottage is near the West side of Wan Li Bridge, and to the North of Baihuatan". The couplet indicates the original location of the cottage.

Tourist: Well, it is indeed desirable!

Gary Li: Let's walk into the cottage. I know that you will find ancient buildings hidden among trees, bamboos and clear steams.

Tourist: That sounds good.

Situational dialogue 4

Context: After sightseeing, the tour group is waiting for an old man who may have lost his way.

Task: answer the questions below.
1. What did Mr Smith want to do during his free time?
2. What does Gary Li think is the reason for Mr Smith's missing?
3. Why doesn't Gary Li agree with Eric's first suggestion?
4. What is Gary Li's suggestion?

Gary Li: Hi, Eric. It's time to go. Are you all here?

Eric: Let me see. No, Mr Smith is missing. He's quite elderly.

Gary Li: Has anyone seen him recently?

Eric: No, he wanted to wander about by himself during his free time.

Gary Li: Oh dear, there are two entrances. I hope he hasn't gone out of and got lost.

Eric: Let me ask some of the group to go and look for him, is that OK?

Gary Li: I don't think so. We may lose everyone or to wait for even more people.

Eric: Yes, maybe. I could go and look for him whilst you escort everyone else to the bus. They can wait on the bus.

Gary Li: Mm... I think it would be better if we ask the staff for help.

Eric: Oh, look, here he comes.
Gary Li: Thank God! Let's go!

Part IV Vocabulary

Textbook	Word stress	Translation
monastery	MO-na-ste-ry	隐修院；修道院；寺院
ancient	AN-cient	古代的；过时的；年老的
primitive	PRI-mi-tive	原始的；简单的；粗糙的；原始人
rebellion	re-BE-llion	谋反；叛乱；反抗；不顺从；叛逆
suppress	su-PPRESS	镇压；禁止；查禁；封锁；抑制
opportunity	o-ppor-TU-ni-ty	时机；机会
classic	CLA-ssic	经典的；传统的；最优秀的；名著
trace	TRACE	追溯；查探；描绘；痕迹
turbulent	TUR-bu-lent	动荡的；混乱的；汹涌的
proclaim	pro-CLAIM	宣布；声明；明确显示
exquisite	ex-QUI-site	精致的；细腻的；高雅的
architecture	AR-chi-tec-ture	建筑风格；建筑式样；架构
belief	be-LIEF	相信；信赖；信仰；教义
attempt	a-TTEMPT	企图；试图；尝试
resign	re-SIGN	辞职；辞去
relic	RE-lic	遗迹；遗风；遗俗；圣人遗物
souvenir	sou-ve-NIR	纪念物；纪念品；礼物
photogenic	pho-to-GE-nic	上镜的；上相的
horizontal	HO-ri-ZON-tal	水平的；地平线的；同一阶层的
couplet	COUP-let	对句；对联

阅读译文

成都武侯祠

　　武侯祠是为了纪念三国时期著名的战略家、政治家诸葛亮而建的。
　　中国有着3600多年有文字记载的历史。它始于商朝（公元前16世纪—公元前11世纪）。整个古代史分为三个阶段。第一阶段是原始社会，历史与假定的前夏王朝（公元前21世纪—公元前16世纪）有很大联系。第二个主要阶段从大约公元前2000年持续到公元前200年，历史可以追溯到夏朝奴隶社会的开始。第三阶段从公元前221年一直延伸到1840年鸦片战争。史书将第三阶段称为封建帝制社会。东汉末年，中国封建社会进入了一个四分五裂的时期。传统上称为三国时期。

> 东汉末年发生了一场农民大起义。许多地方官员成为自治区军阀。他们镇压了叛乱，同时利用这个机会建立了自己的政治和军事力量。最后，军阀们将汉帝国划分为魏、蜀、吴三国。
> 　　有一部中国经典小说叫《三国演义》。这部小说很受欢迎，大多数中国家庭都有一本。这部小说基本上追溯了三国的兴衰，生动地描绘了当时动荡的社会状况。曹操和他的儿子在洛阳建立了魏国。实际上，曹操控制了华北的领土。其他两个竞争对手很快就宣称自己是其他地方的皇帝。都城在南京的吴国占领了长江流域。蜀国控制着四川和中国西南高原的部分地区，它的首都在成都。
> 　　武侯祠与蜀国关系密切，它是为了纪念蜀相诸葛亮而建立的。武乡侯是诸葛亮摄政时授予他的最高官衔。他死后，又被授予了另一个头衔，忠武侯，人们尊称他为武侯。
> 　　如果你喜欢旅行，那就来享受这里的视觉盛宴和人文景观吧。你会惊讶于它精致的建筑和丰富的历史。

Part Ⅴ　Discussion

1. Prepare a presentation to the class on the famous scenic spots you collect in spare time.

2. Work in pairs. The tour leader Eric is asking the local guide Gary Li about a scenic spot. Practice making a conversation with reference to the expressions: Where are we going to visit?/I heard it's.../Where is it located?/Does the name have any special meaning?

3. Work in pairs. The tour leader Eric is trying to make requests on behalf of his tourists to the local guide Gary Li. Practice making a conversation.

Part Ⅵ　Writing

Task：Tour commentary.

The introduction of the city often contains the geographical location, politics, economy, culture, the feature of residents and lifestyle and tourist attraction. The function of introducing the city is not only to offer information to tourists but also to promote the image of the city. The most important thing you have to remember is that you have to pay more attention to create the uniqueness of the city rather than to list the characteristic of the city in detail.

Module 4
Hotel accommodation

Unit 10 | Check in

 Learning objectives

1. Know the procedures of check-in at a hotel.
2. Master the useful expressions about check-in.
3. Know how to help guests to fill out the registration forms.

Part I Warming up

Can you speak out the name of the items below (room type/hotel department/job title)?

_____ _____ _____ _____

_____ _____ _____ _____

_____ _____ _____ _____

"Taking care of your employees and they will take care of your customers."
（当你照顾好你的员工，你的员工就会照顾好你的客人。）

Marriott International founder
——J.W. Marriott

Part II Reading

MARRIOTT

Marriott International is founded by J. Willard and Alice Marriott, and guided by family leadership since 1927. Their principles remain embedded in its culture and everything they do today.

Since 1927, Marriott has attached much significance to the diversity and inclusion. Embracing differences has been in corporated into their daily operations around the world and becomes critical to their success as the largest hospitality company with an ever-growing global portfolio. Diversity and inclusion are fundamental to their main values and strategic business goals. Taking care of people and putting their well-being above everything is in their Company's DNA and their most precious cultural inheritance.

The core values of Marriott International make them who they are. As they change and grow, the beliefs that are most important to them stay the same—putting people first, pursuing excellence, embracing change, acting with integrity and serving the world. Being part of Marriott International means being part of a proud history and a thriving culture.

"Putting people first". It means if they take care of associates, and the associates will take care of the customers. This is their founder's philosophy, which has made Marriott International a great place to work for more than 85 years. Their people-first culture has consistently earned them awards and recognition around the globe. Giving opportunities to associates and make them grow and succeed is part of the company's DNA.

"Pursuing excellence". It means their dedication to the customer should show in everything they do. Marriott's reputation for superior customer service dates back to J. Willard Marriott's original goal for his business: "good food and good service at a fair price." They are so proud of the details—every day, in every destination worldwide.

"Embracing change". Innovation has always been part of the Marriott story. The Marriott family made a crucial contribution to the modern hospitality industry. They're driven to continually challenge the status quo and anticipate the customers' changing needs with new brands, new global locations and new guest experiences.

"Acting with integrity". The way they do business and their own business are equally important in their mind. They hold themselves to uncompromising ethical and legal standards and extend to their day-to-day business conduct, employee policies, supply chain policies, environmental programs and practices and their commitment to human rights and social responsibility.

"Serving the world". Marriott strives to be a force for good. Their sustainability and social impact platform, guides their path to making a positive and sustainable effect wherever they do business.

Marriott International is a Brand Leader, Offering the most powerful portfolio in the loading industry, its 30 brands and 7000+ properties across 131 countries and territories give customers more ways to connect, experience and expand the world.

After reading, please answer the questions below:
1. What are the Core Values of Marriott International?
2. What are the grades of its brand?
3. If you have a chance to work in Marriott International, which brand will you choose? Why?

Part III Listening

Listen to *dialogues* and finish the tasks.
Situational dialogue 1
Context: Shirley is a hotel receptionist; she is ready to help the tour guide Sherry Li to check in.

Task: answer the questions below.
1. Is there any change for the reservation?
2. What does the tour guide show to the receptionist when check-in?
3. Where does the breakfast serve?
4. Does the hotel have emergency instruction? Why does the tour guide tell it to the members?
5. Try to rehearse this dialogue.

Shirley: Good evening. Welcome to our hotel! Are you the tour guide Sherry Li?

Sherry Li: Yes, Nice to meet you.

Shirley: Nice to meet you too. May I reconfirm your reservation. You have made a reservation for ten double rooms and three single rooms, right?

Sherry Li: Yes.

Shirley: Very good. Ma'am so may I have the passports?

Sherry Li: Here you are. 24 in all.

Shirley: Thank you! Here is the rooming list. Please have a check.

Sherry Li: Thank you.

Shirley: Do you have a group visa?

Sherry Li: Yes, we have. Here you are.

Shirley: All right. I'll make a copy of your group visa. Please wait for a moment. (After a while). Thanks for your waiting. Here are the room keys and breakfast vouchers. The buffet breakfast is served from 6:30 to 10:00 a.m. at the western restaurant hall on the second floor. Could you please divide them to the guests?

Sherry Li: Yes, certainly.

Shirley: May I confirm your check-out time? According to your schedules you will check out at 8:30 a.m. on the 21st. Is that right?

Sherry Li: Yes. We would like to change our check-out time to 9:00 tomorrow morning.

Shirley: No problem, Ma'am. What time will you have a morning call?

Eric: The morning call will be 7:30 a.m.

Shirley: I see. 7:30 a.m. on the 21st. Could you please place your luggage in front of your room doors by 8:30 a.m.? The bellman will pick them up. Anything else I can do for you?

Eric: No, thanks.

Shirley: If there is any change, please inform the Front Desk.

Eric: OK. Thank you.

Shirley: Thank you. I hope you'll enjoy your stay with us!

Sherry Li: :(to the group guests)
Good evening, ladies and gentlemen. Attention please. I have delivered the envelopes to you. Please check whether the envelope bears your name.

Your breakfast is buffet tomorrow. It will be served from 6:30 to 10:00 a.m.at the western restaurant hall on the second floor. Please remember to take your breakfast voucher to have breakfast. The morning call is at 7:30 tomorrow morning.

Please remember to take the room card uith you until checking out. After you get to your room, please read the emergency instruction which is on the back of your room door. The nearest emergency exit is shown clearly.

The bellman will deliver your luggage to your rooms soon. If you need any help, don't hesitate to call me. My room number is 1619. I hope you have a good night and a nice sleep. Thank you!

Situational dialogue 2

Context: Shirley is a hotel receptionist; she is at the reception when a guest Eric Smith comes to check in.

Tasks: answer the questions below.

1. Did the guests have a reservation?
2. What does the front desk ask the guests to fill in?
3. What's the exchange rate of euro to RMB?
4. Summarize the procedures of helping guests to check-in.

Shirley: Good morning, Sir. How may I help you?

Eric: Good morning, I'd like to check in.

Shirley: Do you have a reservation?

Eric: Yes, I reserved last week.

Shirley: OK. May I ask your name, please?

Eric: Yes, Eric Smith.

Shirley: Just a moment, please. Let me check our reservation record. (after a while) Thanks for your waiting, Mr. Smith. I've get your record. You have reserved one single room for 2 nights, is that right?

Eric: That's exactly right!

Shirley: Would you please fill out this registration form and check your departure date and the room rate, and sign your name here? Arriving August 10th and departing August 12th, the room rate is RMB 980 yuan per night.

Eric: Yes, that's fine. (fill in the form) Is that OK?

Shirley: Yes, May I have your passport?

Eric: OK, here you are!

Shirley: May I ask how will you be paying?/May I ask how would you like to pay?

Eric: OK, here is my Visa Card, do you accept it?

Shirley: Certainly.

Eric: Oh, Do you exchange euro?

Shirley: Yes, just a moment, please! Let me check today's exchange rate. It's 761 yuan against 100 euro. How much would you like to change?

Eric: 500 euro, please.

Shirley: OK, that's 3805 yuan. Please fill in the exchange memo and sign your name on it.

Eric: Thanks.

Shirley: OK, and do you have any luggage? May I get the bellboy to help you?

Eric: Yes, so kind of you, my bags are quite heavy!

Shirley: No problem. Here is your room key, Mr. Smith. Your room number is 0115, the bellman will show you there in a minute, I hope you will enjoy your stay with us.

Eric: Thank you.

Shirley: You're welcome.

Situational dialogue 3

Context: Bob is a hotel bellboy; the American guest Joyce Li is arriving at the hotel. Bob is helping the guest Joyce with the luggage.

Task: answer the questions below.

1. What's the duty of the bellboy?
2. Is the bellboy important to a hotel? Why?
3. Summarize the procedures of showing guests to the room.

Bob: (Open the vehicle door) Good morning, ma'am. Welcome to SIX SENSES Hotel. Do you have any luggage?

Joyce: Yes, I have a suitcase in the trunk. Thank you.

Bob: You are welcome, ma'am. (after taking the suitcase). One case, right? I'll show you to the front desk, this way, please.

Joyce: OK. Thanks.

Bob: (After check-in) May I have your room number, ma'am? Let me show you to the room.

Joyce: You are so kind. My room is 1916.

Bob: I see, It's a wonderful room with mountain view. It's very beautiful. I hope you will like it.

Joyce: Yes. I will.

Bob: This way please.

Joyce: Wow. The room looks very nice.

Bob: Let me introduce the room facilities for you. Here is the light switch, the wardrobe, and the mini bar. And the panel on the nightstand controls the different devices in the room. By the way, there are two sockets in the bathroom, for 110V and 220V respectively, the voltage here is much lighter than that in the U.S.A. If you want to make an outside call, please dial "0" first. There is a telephone directory on the writing desk. You may read it. This is the remote control. There are sixteen channels including three English programs and a French program. Don't drink the tap water unless it is boiled. And there are two bottles of drinking water in the bathroom, free of charge. What' more, our spa is really good, and you can have a try. If you need anything else, please dial 8. We're always at your service.

Situational dialogue 4

Context: Sarah is a hotel staff; she is showing the guest Joyce Li around the hotel.

Task: discussion

What does the dialogue talk about? And why is it important to introduce your hotel to guests?

Sarah: Good morning, Sherry! How was your stay last night?

Sherry: It's really great, thank you! I just want to ask if there some place I can visit in this hotel?

Sarah: Of course! I have this map for you. If you want to take a walk, you can go to the garden, it is very relaxing there.

Sherry: That sounds good. But is this the only one place where I can go?

Sarah: Of course not. There is a recreation center on the ground floor. You can play the billiards, table tennis, bridge, and go bowling.

Sherry: But, is there a place where I can listen to some music?

Sarah: Oh, there is a music tea house where you can enjoy both classical music such as Beethoven, Bach, Mozart, Liszt, and modern music while you having some Chinese tea or other drinks.

Sherry: Sounds great.

Sarah: Actually, we aim to health and firstly I'll show you to the organic farm in our hotel. You can see all the vegetables and poultry are away from chemicals and fodder. Guests can experience the joy of farming.

Sherry: Wow, I think it must be a kind of good experience.

Sarah: Of course, we have the creative products exhibition room also, there are different kinds of creative products such as the panda pillow, postcard and so on.

Sherry: Wow, you know I love pandas, because I think it must be the cutest animal in this world.

Sarah: Of course, this is our cinema and Yoga room, you can relax yourself with our professional Yoga instructor. They are free for the in house guests.

Sherry: Really? But I want to try the spa first.

Sarah: Of course, no problem. Need I make a reservation for you?
Sherry: Sure, please, Thank you so much!
Sarah: My pleasure and enjoy your spa.

Situational dialogue 5

Context: Joyce Li, a guest in SIX SENSES, wants to travel to the CHINA PANDA VALLEY; she is asking the hotel staff Laura.
Task:
Please help Joyce to draw a map to show the way to the CHINA PANDA VALLEY.

Joyce: Excuse me. Could you tell me the way to the famous panda breeding base in Du jiangyan?
Laura: Good morning, ma'am! You mean the CHINA PANDA VALLEY?
Joyce: I don't know the exact name, but I just know there are so many pandas.
Laura: Yes, I think that is CHINA PANDA VALLEY.
Joyce: OK. How can I get there?
Laura: I got a map for you, don't worry. If you want to go by taxi, it will take 15 minutes and cost you RMB 30 yuan. If you want to take the bus, when you step out of the hotel, turn right and walk for about 2 minutes, you will get to a bus stop. You can take Bus No. A and only eight stops from here. And it will take 30 minutes and just cost 2 yuan. Please get your small change prepared before you take the bus.
Joyce: Thank you very much. But, can I see the CHINA PANDA VALLEY just immediately after I get off?
Laura: Yes, of course. It is close to the stop, you can't miss it.
Joyce: Got it, thank you so much.
Laura: You are welcome. Howe a nice day.
Joyce: You too, bye.

Part IV Vocabulary

Textbook	Word stress	Translation
embed	em-BED	把…嵌入，栽种，深留
diversity	di-VER-si-ty	多样性，差异，分歧
inclusion	in-CLU-sion	包含，内含物
associate	a-SSO-ci-ate	联盟，同事
critical	CRI-ti-cal	批评的，关键的，严重的
portfolio	port-FO-li-o	公文包，代表作品集

Textbook	Word stress	Translation
inheritance	in-HE-ri-tance	继承，遗传，遗产
pillar	PI-llar	（组织、制度等的）核心
legacy	LE-ga-cy	遗产，遗赠
vibrant	VI-brant	振动的，响亮的，充满生气的
integrity	in-TEG-ri-ty	正直，诚实，完整，健全
property	PRO-per-ty	特性，属性，地产，所有权
territory	TE-rri-to-ry	领土，版图，势力范围
reconfirm	re-con-FIRM	重新确认
rooming list	ROOMING list	分房名单
group visa	group VISA	团队签证
voucher	VOU-cher	证件，凭证，收据，证人
schedule	SCHE-dule	时刻表，进度表，计划
reservation	re-ser-VA-tion	保留，预订，预约
registration form	re-gi-STRA-tion form	登记表
departure	de-PAR-ture	离开，离去，起程
room rate	ROOM rate	房价
exchange rate	ex-CHANGE rate	汇率，兑换率
trunk	TRUNK	汽车车尾的行李箱
exhibition	exhi-BI-tion	陈列，展览，展览品
wardrobe	WAR-drobe	衣柜，衣橱；（个人）行头
master switch	MAS-ter switch	总开关
panel	PA-nel	（门、墙等上面的）控制板
socket	SOC-ket	插座，灯座
voltage	VOL-tage	电压，伏特数
electric shaver	E-LEC-tric-sha-ver	电动剃须刀
telephone directory	TE-le-phone di-REC-to-ry	电话号簿
writing desk	WRI-ting desk	写字桌，书写台
remote control	re-MOTE con-TROL	遥控器，远程控制
program list	PRO-gram list	节目清单
billiards	BI-lliards	台球，桌球，弹子球
poultry	POUL-try	家禽
chemicals	CHE-mi-cals	化学药品
fodder	fod-der	饲料

阅读译文

万豪国际集团

豪国际集团由J.威拉德和爱丽丝·马里奥特于1927年创立,在家族式管理的一路引领下,创始人所坚持的原则深植于企业文化之中,清晰地引领着他们的前进方向。

自1927年以来,万豪一直十分重视多元化与包容性。认同差异已融入他们在全球各地的日常业务当中,并在使其成为超群的酒店管理企业,在不断发展全球品牌方面发挥了重要作用。多元化与包容性构成了万豪的核心价值观和商业策略目标的基础。予人关爱、增进福祉,是他们宝贵的文化传承。

万豪的核心价值观使他们拥有了现在的辉煌成绩。尽管经历着不断的发展变迁,但他们重要的核心信念却从未改变,即以人为本、追求卓越、勇于创新、诚实正直及感恩回报。加入万豪国际集团,就意味着成为这一辉煌历史和繁荣文化的一部分。

"以人为本"——照顾好员工,员工才能照顾好顾客。85年来,万豪国际集团在创始人J. Willard Marriott经营理念的指导下成为备受赞誉的理想工作场所。"以人为本"的企业文化为他们赢得了无数奖项以及全球范围的广泛认可。为员工提供发展和成功机会则是公司的核心组成部分。

"追求卓越"——对客户的专注体现在我们所做的每一件事上。万豪在卓越的客户服务方面的卓著声誉可追溯至J.Willard为万豪业务制定的初始目标:"精致美食、卓越服务、合理价格"。在世界各地的每一个目的地,他们每时每刻都在为这些细节而倍感自豪。

"勇于创新"——创新一直以来都是万豪发展历史中不可分割的一部分。而万豪家族在塑造现代酒店业的过程中亦功不可没。他们始终通过新的品牌、新的全球地点以及新的顾客体验来不断挑战现状,并准确预测变化迅速的客户需求。

"诚实正直"——在他们看来业务方式与业务内容是同等重要的。他们始终严于律己,以一丝不苟的态度奉行严格的道德和法律标准。他们还将这一原则延伸到日常业务行为、员工政策、供应链政策、环境计划和实践中,并致力于维护人权、承担社会责任的坚定承诺中。

"感恩回报"——服务精神要使公司变得更加强大。在他们的可持续发展及社会影响力平台"善行360度"的引领下,万豪为业务所在的各个领域创造可持续发展的积极影响。

万豪是备受认可的酒店行业领导品牌,拥有非凡卓越的品牌组合,30个大品牌旗下7000多家酒店覆盖131个国家和地区,为宾客呈献更多选择去感受、体验并探索世界。

Part V Discussion

1. How to make room reservations for guests?

2. Suppose you are a bellman; you have received a group of 18 foreign travelers. How to help them with the luggage?

3. How to do up-selling to a businessman?

4. How to change US dollars into RMB for guests? (exchange rate: ＄100 = ￥797 Yuan)

5. Imagine you were a staff in SIX SENSES, how can you introduce the way to Mt. Qingcheng to foreign guests?

Part Ⅵ Writing

According to what you have learned in this unit, try to make a registration form and foreign currency exchanging memo with your partner.

Unit 11 | F & B Service

  Learning objectives

1. Know the procedures of F & B service at a hotel.
2. Master the useful expressions about F & B service.
3. Know how to help guests to make reservations, welcome guests, take orders, serve the dishes and pay the bill.

Part I Warming up

Can you speak out the name of the items below?

_____   _____   _____   _____

_____   _____   _____   _____

_____   _____   _____   _____

"Well done is better than well said."
（说得好不如做得好。）

——Benjamin Franklin

Module 4   Hotel accommodation   085

Part II   Reading

Two cities tussle over who makes the tastiest Sichuan hotpot

Chengdu, the capital of Sichuan province, has an ancient rivalry with Chongqing, a city to its south-east. Residents of Both cities share a love of spice-laden Sichuan cuisine, which recently has conquered Chinese palates. But they are at war over which has the best Sichuan hotpot—a type of diy-cooking that involves boiling vegetables and slices of meat in a communal broth with chilies and numbing peppercorns. A private museum in Chongqing makes the case for Chongqing-style hotpot, and Chengdu is playing catch-up. In January the city sold a plot of land on condition that the developer build a hotpot museum on part of it. The two cities are among many in China with their own styles of hotpot. The stories behind these dishes reveal how different regions like to see themselves. Chongqing's is said to highlight the ingenuity of the proletariat. Other places describe their hotpots as the sophisticated food of emperors. But Sichuan-style broths are the most commonly savoured in China. China has around 350, 000 hotpot restaurants. About 40, 000 are in the Chongqing region alone.

The more adventurous tastes of younger Chinese are fuelling demand. They have little time to cook at home and are unburdened by child-care duties. Round-the-clock restaurants are sprouting up to allow leisurely feasting.

TASK:
According to the text, discuss with your partners about hotpot in Chongqing and Chengdu.

Part III   Listening

Listen to *dialogues* and finish the tasks.
Situational dialogue 1
Context: Shirley is answering the phone from Eric Smith who wants to reserve a table.

Task:
1. Discuss with your group members to find out the procedures of table reservation.
2. Try to rehearse this dialogue.

Shirley: Good morning, SIX SENSES! Shirley speaking. What can I do for you?
Eric: Good morning. I'd like to have dinner in your restaurant tonight. Can I reserve a table?
Shirley: Certainly, sir. What time would you like to have your dinner?

Eric: Around 6:00 p.m..

Shirley: OK, sir. For how many guests?

Eric: Just 2, my wife and me.

Shirley: Fine! I will reserve the table for 2 at 6:00 p.m., sir. May I have your name and telephone number?

Eric: Sure. Eric, Eric Smith. And my telephone number is 13687930472.

Shirley: OK. Mr Smith, do you prefer smoking or non-smoking area?

Eric: Non-smoking, please. And it is more important if you get us a table by the window. It's our anniversary and I'd like it to be special.

Shirley: Wow, we will try our best. So, you reserved a table for 2 in the non-smoking area by the window, and under the name of Eric Smith, and your telephone number is 13687930472. Is that right?

Eric: Yes, you are right.

Shirley: OK, we are looking forward to having you with us tonight, Mr Smith.

Eric: Thank you. Goodbye.

Shirley: Goodbye and have a nice day.

Situational dialogue 2

Context: Oven is greeting and seating guests-Mr.and Mrs.Smith.

Tasks:

1. Discuss with your group members to find out the procedures of greeting and seating guests.

2. Try to rehearse this dialogue.

Oven: Good evening, Sir. Welcome to our restaurant! Do you have a reservation?

Smith: Yes. Under the name of Mr. Eric Smith.

Oven: Eric Smith, let me check. Part of 2, is that correct?

Smith: Yes, that's right.

Oven: Let me show you to your table, this way, please?

Smith: Thank you!

Oven: Mr. Smith, this is your table. Do you like it?

Smith: What a nice table! Thank you so much.

Oven: My pleasure! Please take your seat. Here is our menu and the wine list. Excuse me, sir. Would you like a bottle of sparkling or still water?

Smith: Sparkling water, please!

Oven: Please wait a moment. OK. Here is your sparkling water. Please take your time, and I'll be back quickly to take your orders.

Situational dialogue 3

Context: Oven is helping guests-Mr. and Mrs.Smith to take orders.

Module 4 Hotel accommodation 087

Tasks:
1. Discuss with your group members to find out the procedures of taking orders.
2. Try to rehearse this dialogue.

Oven: Good evening, are we ready to order now?
Smith: Yes. Can you give us some recommendation?
Oven: Certainly! I am happy to recommend the *FISH AND CHIPS*. It tastes delicious, and its today's special. Our chef is from the coast and is very good at seafood. So, I'm sure it is absolutely fabulous, and you will like it.
Smith: It does sound fantastic. However, I've heard your Beijing Roast Duck is very famous.
Oven: Oh, Yes! But I'm so sorry, and it has been sold out.
Smith: What a pity! Maybe we'll try the *FISH AND CHIPS*.
Oven: OK! Is there anything else? Maybe I could introduce you one of our fine appetizers- SALAD.
Smith: Yes, sure!
Oven: And what kind of soup would you like? We have *TOMATO SOUP* and *SPICY SOUP*.
Smith: We don't like spicy, just *TOMATO SOUP*, please!
Oven: That's OK, would you guys like something to drink?
Smith: Yeah, *white wine*, *please*.
Shirley: OK, how about the desserts?
Smith: Tiramisu. Thank you!
Oven: OK. Let me repeat your order. That's *THE GREEN SALADS, TOMATO SOUPS, THE FISH AND CHIPS, and TIRAMISU*, All for 2, and a bottle of *white wine*. Right?
Smith: Yes, that's right. Thank you.
Oven: You are welcome. Your meal will be ready soon.

Situational dialogue 4

Context: Oven is serving the food for guests-Mr.and Mrs.Smith.
Tasks:
1. Discuss with your group members to find out the procedures of serving food.
2. Try to rehearse this dialogue.

Oven: Excuse me. Your meal is ready. This is your appetizer-*SALAD*.
Smith: Thank you!
Oven: How was it, Sir?
Smith: It was really good! I like it so much.
Oven: I'm so glad to hear that. May I take the plates away?
Smith: Sure!
Oven: Would you like me to serve you the soup now?

Smith: Yes, please!

Oven: It is hot. Be careful!

Smith: Thank you.

Oven: This is the *FISH AND CHIPS you ordered*. Enjoy.

Smith: Thank you! Can I have some pepper?

Oven: Certainly, Sir! Here you are, Sir. Bon Appétit.

Oven: Excuse me, Sir. Do you want some more wine?

Smith: Yes, please. The food is really fabulous, by the way.

Oven: Sir, do you want your desserts now?

Smith: Sure!

Oven: This is your Tiramisu.

Smith: Thank you!

Oven: You are welcome coffee or Tea?

Mrs. Smith: Latte, please.

Mr. Smith: Espresso, please.

Oven: Please wait a minute.

Smith: Thank you.

Oven: Enjoy.

Smith: Thanks.

Situational dialogue 5

Context: Oven is helping the guests-Mr.and Mrs.Smith to settle the bill.

Tasks:

1. Discuss with your group members to find out the procedures of settling the bill.
2. Try to rehearse this dialogue.

Oven: Excuse me, Sir?

Smith: May I have my bill, please?

Oven: Certainly! Sir. Please wait a moment, and I'll be back very soon.

Oven: How was your dinner tonight with us, Sir?

Smith: Wonderful! Your food is delicious, and your service is excellent.

Oven: Thank you so much! And here is your bill. It totals 1000 yuan, including tax and service charge. How would you like to pay for it.

Smith: OK, do you accept dollars?

Oven: Sorry, we only accept credit card, Alipay and WeChat.

Smith: OK! Maybe I can pay with Alipay.

Oven: Certainly! Please scan the QR code here.

Smith: Is that ok?

Oven: Yes, Sir! This is your receipt and invoice, please have a look.

Smith: That right, No problem.
Oven: Thanks!
Smith: Goodbye.

Part IV Vocabulary & Notes

Textbook	Word stress	Translation
rivalry	RI-val-ry	竞争；对抗；竞赛
cousin	COU-sin	堂兄弟姊妹；表兄弟姊妹；对等物
pompous	POM-pous	浮夸的；爱炫耀的；自大的
hothead	HOT-head	急性子的人；鲁莽的人
dweller	DWE-ller	居民；居住者
spice-laden	spice-LA-den	辣味十足的
communal	com-MU-nal	公共的；公社的
broth	BROTH	肉汤；（火锅）高汤
chilli	CHI-lli	红辣椒
numbing	NU-mbing	使麻木的；使失去感觉的
peppercorn	PE-pper-corn	干胡椒
catch-up	CATCH-up	追赶…以达到同样的水平
ingenuity	in-ge-NU-i-ty	足智多谋；心灵手巧
proletariat	pro-le-TA-riat	工人阶级；尤指无产阶级
savour	SA-vour	细品；享用（食物）
fuel	FUEL	加强；激起；为…添加燃料
unburdened	un-BUR-dened	无牵累的
reservation	re-ser-VA-tion	保留；预订；预约
anniversary	an-ni-VER-sa-ry	周年纪念日
recommendation	re-com-men-DA-tion	推荐；建议；可取之处
fabulous	FA-bu-lous	极好的；（美貌）惊人的
appetizer	A-ppe-ti-zer	开胃品；开胃菜
tiramisu	ti-ra-mi-SU	提拉米苏
pepper	pe-pper	胡椒；辣椒；胡椒粉
ladle	LADLE	长柄勺；（用勺）舀或盛（食物）
hesitate	HE-si-tate	犹豫；踌躇；不愿；停顿
credit card	CRE-dit card	信用卡，签账卡
Alipay	ALI-pay	支付宝
WeChat	WE-chat	微信

Notes

1. tussle with sb. over sth. (fight with sb over sth) 与某人争夺某物
2. have a rivalry with sb. 与某人是竞争关系
3. accuse sb. of doing sth. 指责某人做某事
4. play catch-up 追赶
5. a plot of 一块（土地）
6. on condition that 在…条件下
7. sprout up 涌现
8. describe sb./sth. as... 把…描述为…
9. commonly adv. 一般地；通常地；普通地
10. 中国八大菜系

Sichuan Cuisine 川菜   Guangdong Cuisine 粤菜
Shandong Cuisine 鲁菜   Fujian Cuisine 闽菜
Hunan Cuisine 湘菜   Zhejiang Cuisine 浙菜
Anhui Cuisine 徽菜   Jiangsu Cuisine 苏菜

11. QR code (Quick Response Code) 二维码

阅读译文

两座城市争论谁的四川火锅最美味

四川省省会成都有一个宿命的对手，那就是位于其东南方的重庆。这两座城市都喜爱辣劲十足的川菜。近些年来，川菜已经征服了中国人民的味蕾。但现在，两座城市为谁的四川火锅最正宗而争得不可开交。四川火锅是一种自助式的烹饪方法，食客们共用一口锅，汤中配以辣椒和花椒，加入各种蔬菜和肉片烹煮。除了成都和重庆，中国还有许多城市火锅风格各不相同。这些佳肴背后的故事揭示了不同地区眼中的自己。有人说，重庆火锅彰显了劳动人民的创造力；有些地方则把当地的火锅描述为御用的珍馐。但在中国最受欢迎的，还要数川式火锅。全中国大约有35万家火锅店，仅重庆地区就有近4万家。中国的年轻人更敢于尝试新口味，这刺激了火锅的需求。他们通常没时间在家里做饭，也还没有照顾孩子的重担。24小时营业的餐厅如雨后春笋般涌现，供人们"巴适"地大快朵颐。

Part V Discussion

1. Suppose the tour guide, who reserved the dinner of 20 persons at your restaurant, was stuck in the traffic jam and would be late for 1hour. What would you do after you heard this?

2. Choose a Chinese dish you know very well and introduce it to the guests to make them salivate.

3. To practice how to settle the bill in cash with your partner.

Part VI Writing

According to what you have learned in this unit, try to make a menu of your own restaurant and practice how to serve your guests.

Unit 12 | Housekeeping Service

Learning objectives

1. Know the procedures of HSKP service at a hotel.
2. Master the useful expressions about HSKP service.
3. Know how to help guests to do housekeeping, introduce laundry service, deal with guests' problems and do the room service.

Part I Warming up

Can you speak out the name of the items below?

_____ _____ _____ _____

_____ _____ _____ _____

_____ _____ _____ _____

"Life is like riding a bicycle. To keep your balance, you must keep moving."
（生活就像骑自行车一样，为了保持平衡，你必须不断前进。）

——Albert Einstein

Part II Reading

IHG, (InterContinental Hotels Group) is a global organization with a broad portfolio of 16 hotel brands that operates 5,918 hotels (883, 364 rooms) IHG supports each property around the world by balancing regional leadership with local, personalized service. With teams spreading throughout the world, in order to make sure that all IHG branded hotels can get hands-on support to fit their market and guest needs, IHG sets the regional offices in major markets around the world, including the global headquarters in Denham, England, the Americas office in Atlanta,

Georgia, and regional offices in Singapore and Shanghai.

The History of IHG:

1777: William Bass opens a brewery in Burton-on-Trent, UK. And then IHG®'s story starts here, because Bass begins a journey from a local brewery to global hospitality player, acquiring along the way and develops into a world-famous hotel brand.

1946: Hospitality begins to take flight. Pan American Airways founder, Juan Trippe, founds the InterContinental® brand, devoting to provide luxury accommodation at the end of every flight.

1952: Holiday Inn opens its doors in Memphis, Tennessee. On a family trip to Washington DC, businessman Kemmons Wilson has the idea of providing the comfortable and affordable accommodation they could trust to the travelling families. Starting in Memphis, his vision would become a reality in a big way.

1961: Bass acquires pubs owner Mitchells & Butlers. This is the first acquisitions for Bass, during the 1960s, He acquires many other well-known regional pub and brewing companies across the UK.

1984: Holiday Inn is China's first international hotel brand. The openning of the Holiday Inn® Lido in Beijing brings international branded hotels to Greater China for the first time.

1988: Bass makes its way into the hotel industry. The acquisition of Holiday Inn International (excluding North America) represented the first significant step by Bass to gain a foothold in the lodging industry.

1998: Bass adds InterContinental to its growing hotel portfolio. Bass buys the InterContinental Hotels & Resorts brand and takes Juan Trippe's vision to each part of the world.

2000: Bass swaps beer for hotels. Bass acquires Southern Pacific Hotels Corporation in Australia and US-based hotel management company, Bristol Hotels & Resorts Inc. Meanwhile Bass's brewing operations, and the name Bass, are bought by Interbrew (now AB InBev). The deal re-shaped the UK's brewing industry and paved the way for the conglomerate to refocus on hotels and global hospitality.

2003: IHG is born. In April 2003, Six Continents plc splits into two, creating a separate hotels and soft drinks company named InterContinental Hotels Group plc (IHG), and a retail business called Mitchells & Butlers plc. IHG becomes a standalone company from then on.

2016: IHG opens its 5,000th hotel. Consolidating its position as a world leader in hospitality, IHG reaches a milestone with the opening of its 5,000th hotel - the Hotel Indigo® Lower East Side in New York City.

TASK:

1. According to the text, write down both the Chinese and English name of IHG's each brand.

2. Find out more information about IHG and share with your group members.

Module 4　Hotel accommodation　095

Part Ⅲ　Listening

Listen to *dialogues* and finish the tasks.

Situational dialogue 1

Context: Shirley is helping guest-Mr. Smith to set the room up.

Tasks:

1. Discuss with your group members about how to decorate the rooms according to different themes.

2. Try to rehearse this dialogue.

Shirley: Good morning, Mr. Smith. This is the housekeeper Shirley from SIX SENSES hotel. We heard that tomorrow is your wedding anniversary with your wife. You want to give your wife a surprise. So how would you like to decorate your room?

Smith: My wife loves red roses, and we met because of the panda. It's a romantic memory. Do you have red roses?

Shirley: Certainly, we can provide red roses to decorate your room. We will give you a pair of panda dolls as small gifts. The two pandas represent you and your wife, respectively.

Smith: Fantastic. Thank you so much. I'm looking forward to seeing it.

Shirley: I'm sure you won't be disappointed. Good-bye.

Smith: Good-bye.

Situational dialogue 2

Context: Shirley is trying to help Eric to do the housekeeping.

Task:

1. Discuss with your group members to find out the procedures of housekeeping.

2. Try to rehearse this dialogue.

Shirley: (Knocking at the door) Housekeeping. May I come in?

Eric: Oh, I was going to take a bath. Could you come back in half an hour?

Shirley: Certainly, sir. See you.

...

Shirley: (Knocking at the door) Housekeeping. May I come in?

Eric: Come in, please.

Shirley: Good morning, Mr. White. I'm sorry to disturb you. Would you like to have your room to be made now?

Eric: Yes, please. Could you start with the bath? I've just taken a bath, and it is quite a mess.

Shirley: Certainly.

Eric: Thank you. (After the cleaning)

Shirley: Mr.White, your room has already been made. Is there anything else I can do for you?
Eric: Oh, the hairdryer doesn't work.
Shirley: So sorry about that. I'll get another one for you right away.
Eric: Thank you, so kind of you.
Shirley: You are welcome. Have a nice day.

Situational dialogue 3

Context: There is something wrong with the water tap at Mr. Smith's room. Shirley is dealing with it.

Tasks:
1. Discuss with your group members to find out the procedures of dealing with guests' problems.
2. Try to rehearse this dialogue.

Shirley: Good morning, Shirley speaking, how may I assist you?
Smith: The water tap in my bathroom is broken. I've turned off the water tap, but the water keeps running.
Shirley: I'm sorry about that, Mr Smith. I will call the engineer to repair it immediately. Moreover, we do apologize for the inconvenience. Would you mind our engineer coming into your room now?
Smith: Not at all.
Shirley: Thank you. Mr Smith. Just a moment, our engineer is coming in 5 minutes.
Smith: Thank you!
...
Shirley: Engineering? This is Shirley from housekeeping. The water tap in room 8018 is broken, and the guest is waiting for the service in the room.
Oven: OK, Shirley, we got it. We will go and have a check now.
Shirley: Thank you so much.
...
Oven: (Knocking at the door) Engineering. May I come in?
Smith: Come in, please. Thanks for coming, as you can see, the water tap in the bathroom is not working.
Oven: OK, please let me check first. Perhaps I'll replace it with a new one. Yeah, you see. The water tap works now.
Smith: Wow. Great! Thanks a lot.
Oven: My pleasure, I hope you have a nice day. Good-bye.
Smith: Good-bye.

Situational dialogue 4

Context: Shirley is introducing laundry service to guest-Mr. Smith.

Module 4　Hotel accommodation

Tasks:

1. Discuss with your group members to find out the procedures of introducing laundry service.

2. Try to rehearse this dialogue.

Shirley: (Knocking at the door) Housekeeping. Do you have any laundry, sir?
Smith: Oh, yes, I do! Could you please help to collect them?
Shirley: Of course, I can. Have you filled the laundry form?
Smith: No, where is it?
Shirley: You can find it in your closet.
Smith: Oh, I see. Wait a moment, let me finish it.
Shirley: OK, done!. Here are my laundry and the form.
Shirley: Thank you. Your laundry will be sent back before 6 p.m. tomorrow.
Smith: OK. How much I need to pay for this?
Shirley: The price for cleaning a shirt is 50 yuan. You have two shirts, so you need to pay 100 yuan plus 10% service charge and 6% tax. It totals RMB 116 yuan.
Smith: OK, I see. Thank you.
Shirley: You are welcome.

Part IV　Vocabulary & Notes

Textbook	Word stress	Translation
portfolio	port-FO-li-o	（证券投资）组合；部长（职位）
hands-on	HANDS-on	实际动手操作的；即时的
headquarter	HEAD-quar-ter	将…的总部设在；总部
brewery	BREW-e-ry	酿酒厂；啤酒厂
pub	PUB	酒馆；客栈
acquire	a-CQUIRE	获得；取得；学到
acquisition	a-cqui-SI-tion	获得；购置物；获得物；收购
represented	re-pre-SEN-ted	代表；体现；作为…的代表
significant	sig-NI-fi-cant	重要的；显著的；有重大意义的
foothold	FOOT-hold	立足处；稳固地位；据点
conglomerate	con-GLO-me-rate	企业；集团
split	SPLIT	划分；分歧；裂缝；劈叉
standalone	STAN-da-lone	单独的；独立的
cementing	ce-MEN-ting	粘牢；巩固；在…上抹水泥
milestone	MILE-stone	里程碑；划时代事件
decorate	DE-co-rate	装饰；点缀；粉刷；布置
anniversary	an-ni-VER-sa-ry	周年纪念日

Textbook	Word stress	Translation
provide	pro-VIDE	提供；供给；供应
represent	re-pre-SENT	表现；象征；代表；扮演
respectively	re-SPEC-tive-ly	各自、分别地
fantastic	fan-TAS-tic	极好的；很大的；怪诞的
disappointed	dis-a-PPOIN-ted	失望的；沮丧的；失意的
praise	PRAISE	赞扬；称赞；崇拜；赞词
apologize	a-PO-lo-gize	道歉；认错；辩解；辩护
inconvenience	in-con-VE-nience	不方便；麻烦；为难之处
maintenance	MAIN-te-nance	维持；保持；保养；维修
replace	re-PLACE	替换；代替；把…放回原位
laundry	LAUN-dry	洗衣店；洗好的/待洗的衣服
ironed	I-roned	熨烫的；熨平的
damage	DA-mage	损害；毁坏
tax	TAX	税；税额

Notes

1. swap A for B　用 B 替换 A，调换（过来）
2. pave the way for...　为 ... 铺平道路
3. embarking on　开始

阅读译文

洲际酒店集团

洲际酒店集团（IHG）是一家世界领先的国际酒店集团，拥有16个酒店品牌，管理着5,918家(883,364间客房)酒店。IHG通过平衡区域领导地位和当地个性化服务来支持全球各地的每一家酒店。随着团队遍布世界各地，为了确保所有IHG品牌酒店都能得到满足其市场和客人需求的即时支持。IHG在世界各地的主要市场设有区域办事处，包括在英格兰Denham的全球总部，在佐治亚州亚特兰大的美洲办事处，以及在新加坡和中国上海的区域办事处。

IHG的历史：

1777年，威廉•巴斯在英国的波顿开了一家啤酒厂。IHG的故事从这里开始，因为巴斯开始了从当地酿酒厂到全球酒店业者的旅程，一路收购、发展成了世界著名的酒店品牌。

1946年，酒店业开始腾飞。泛美航空公司创始人胡安•特里普(Juan Trippe)创立了洲际品牌，致力于在每次航班结束时能为客人提供豪华住宿。

1952年，假日酒店在美国的田纳西州孟菲斯开业。商人凯蒙斯·威尔逊（Kemmons Wilson）在华盛顿特区的一次家庭旅行中萌生了一个想法，就是为旅行的家庭提供可以信赖的舒适、实惠的住宿。从孟菲斯开始，他的愿景将在很大程度上成为现实（他后来在美国田纳西州孟菲斯开设了第一家假日酒店）。

　　1961年，巴斯收购了米切尔和巴特勒（Mitchells & Butlers）的酒吧。这是巴斯的第一次收购，20世纪60年代，又收购了英国很多著名的地区性酒吧和酿酒公司。

　　1984年，假日酒店是中国第一家国际酒店品牌。丽都假日酒店在北京的开业是第一次将国际酒店品牌引入大中华区。

　　1988年，巴斯进军酒店业。收购假日酒店品牌（不包括北美地区）是巴斯在酒店业站稳脚跟的第一步。

　　1998年，巴斯将洲际酒店纳入其不断增长的酒店组合中。巴斯收购了洲际酒店和度假村品牌，并将胡安·特里普的愿景带到全球各地。

　　2000年，巴斯用啤酒换酒店。巴斯收购了澳大利亚的南太平洋酒店公司（Southern Pacific Hotels Corporation）和总部位于美国的酒店管理公司——布里斯托尔酒店和度假村公司（Bristol Hotels&Resorts Inc.）。与此同时，巴斯的酿酒业务以及巴斯的名字被英特布鲁啤酒集团 Interbrew（现为百威英博）收购。这笔交易重新塑造了英国的酿酒行业，并为该集团重新将目光投向酒店和全球酒店业铺平了道路。

　　2003年，洲际酒店集团诞生。2003年4月，六洲酒店集团一分为二，变成了一家独立的酒店和软饮料公司[即洲际酒店集团（IHG）]和一个零售业公司[米切尔和巴特勒公司（Mitchells & Butlers）]。从此，IHG就成了一家独立的公司。

　　2016年，洲际酒店集团的第5000家酒店开业。洲际酒店集团的第5000家酒店——纽约东城英迪格酒店的盛大开业巩固了IHG在酒店业的世界领先地位。

Part V　Discussion

　　Suppose you were the clerk in SIX SENSES hotel. There is a boy trying to propose to his girlfriend. In order to enliven the atmosphere, you would like to organize some games. You turn to your group members for help. How would you like to do for this?

Part VI　Writing

　　According to this unit, try to make a laundry list and practice how to introduce it to your guests.

Unit 13 Check out

Learning objectives

1. Know the procedures of check-out at a hotel.
2. Master the useful expressions about check-out.
3. Know how to help guests to make the last impression to be the last impression.

Part I Warming up

Which hotel groups do the following hotel signs belong to?

"The past cannot be changed. The future is yet in your power."
（过去无法被改变，但将来仍在你的掌握之中。）

———Unknown

Part II　Reading

　　The AccorHotels group's 'Iconic A' monogram means "The seal of excellence of the group", fuses the letter A with the bernache which is the historical emblem of the group.

　　The art of hospitality has no bounds. It extends beyond walls, to spark inspired experiences everywhere. The AccorHotels group dare to reimagine the hospitality, industry: it is not as a place or service, but infinite connected moments, no matter the guests want to live, work, or play. They are shaping a future where travelling unlocks a life lived limitlessly. Where powerful brands gives exceptional experiences and value, talent and passion demonstrate a welcoming human touch. Where innovation continually expands boundaries, and a commitment to sustainability protect our only planet. That's why they have created a holistic ecosystem around the consumer, and the innovative services and solutions to power it all. Because the future belongs to those who design it, and the Accor has been working on bringing guests to this beautiful future. They want to be such a pioneer.

　　The AccorHotels group's 50 brands (of which 38 hospitality Brands from luxury to economy) welcome guests to over 100 countries throughout the world, in over 4, 800 hotels (704, 000 rooms) for the most unforgettable staying. From luxury to economy, from aparthotels to thalasso, make the most of a wide choice of destinations to compose guests' vacations, live their dreams and rediscover the meaning of world travel. There are about 280, 000 employees working in Accor Brands.

The History of the AccorHotels:
1967: The first Novotel hotel opened in Lille, France.
1974: The first Ibis Hotel opened in Bordeaux, France.
1975: Merger and acquisition of the Mercure Brand.
1980: Acquisition of SOFITEL.
1984: The first Novotel hotel in China opened.
1990: Acquisition of Motel 6 in the USA and Lenotre.
2001: The first Ibis hotel in China opened.
2007: AccorHotels relaunches Pullman.
2008: Creation of the MGallery brand.
2012: 500th hotel in Asia-Pacific region.
2013: AccorHotels opens 100th Novotel property in Ohuket.
2014: AccorHotels acquires the SEBEL.
2015: Launching strategic cooperation with China Lodging Group (Huazhu).

2016: Acquisition of Onefinestay, the world leader in luxury private residential leasing markets. Launching strategic cooperation with Banyan Tree.

2017: Former French president Nicolas Sarkozy joins AccorHotels International Strategy Committee. Acquisition of Rixos Verychic.

2018: Acquisition of Movenpick, Mantis, Tribe.

2019: Unvells new lifestyle loyalty program.

The Brands of the AccorHotels:

Live

Luxury	Premium	Midscale	Economy
RAFFLES / SLS	mantis / ANGSANA	mantra	BreakFree
ORIENT EXPRESS / SO	25h	NOVOTEL	ibis
BANYAN TREE / SOFITEL	M GALLERY / HYDE	Mercure	ibis STYLES
DELANO / THE HOUSE OF ORIGINALS	21c / MÖVENPICK	adagio	ibis budget
LEGEND / RIXOS	Art Series / GRAND MERCURE	MAMA SHELTER	JO&JOE
Fairmont / onefinestay	MONDRIAN / PEPPERS	TRIBE	hotelF1
	pullman / THE SEBEL		
	swissôtel		

Work | Play | Business accelerators

Work	Play	Distribution	Experience	Operations
nextdoor	DISRUPTIVE	d-edge	JOHN PAUL	adoria
MAMAWORKS	POTEL CHABOT	GEKKO		ASTORE
	PARIS SOCIETY	VERYCHIC		
		ResDiary		

TASK:

1. If you have a chance to work in the AccorHotels, which brand will you choose? Why?
2. Find out more information about the AccorHotels and share with your partners.

Module 4 Hotel accommodation 103

Part III   Listening

Listen to *dialogues* and finish the tasks.

Situational dialogue 1

Context: Shirley is helping guest-Mr. Smith to check out.

Tasks:
1. Discuss with your group members about how to help guests check out.
2. Try to rehearse this dialogue.

Shirley: Good morning, sir. What can I do for you?

Smith: Good morning. I want to check out now.

Shirley: OK. May I have your name and room number, please?

Smith: Eric Smith, Room 0115.

Shirley: Just a moment, please. I'll print out the bill for you.

...

Shirley: Sorry to have kept you waiting, sir. Here is your bill, It totals 2156 yuan, including a 10% service charge. Please have a look.

Smith: That's right. Thank you.

Shirley: Mr Smith, you had paid an advanced deposit of 2000 yuan when you checked in, right?

Smith: Yes.

Shirley: OK, there's still 156 yuan short, how would you like to pay?

Smith: I'd like to pay for my credit card. Here you are.

Shirley: Let me swipe it. Please sign your name on this printout, Mr Smith.

Smith: OK, is that correct?

Shirley: Yes, here is your credit card and the receipt. And how was everything here?

Smith: The room was great. The beds were comfortable, and we weren't expecting our fridge.

Shirley: I'm glad you liked it. Hope to see you again! Have a safe trip, Sir.

Smith: Thank you so much!

Shirley: You are welcome.

Situational dialogue 2

Context: The Concierge staff Oven is calling a taxi for the guest-Mr. and Mrs Smith.

Tasks:
1. Discuss with your group members about how to call a taxi for the guests.
2. Try to rehearse this dialogue.

Oven: Good morning, sir. How may I help you?

Smith: I wanna know how far it is to take a taxi to the airport and how much it will cost.

Oven: oh, it's about 60 kilometers away and takes about 1.5 hours by taxi to the Chengdu Shuangliu International Airport. And perhaps will cost RMB 300 yuan.

Smith: Oh, it's a little expensive.

Oven: That's true. But perhaps I can help you to call a DiDi taxi. It is much cheaper and very safe, because we can check the route and your location once you get on.

Smith: Cool. So kind of you. Could you tell me how to call it?

Oven: Certainly! Firstly, please download the DiDi App, then to fill out your information and apply for an account, finally to add an emergency contact person and bind it to your WeChat wallet.

Smith: Just a minute!

...

Smith: Is that correct?

Oven: Yes, great! So, you can call a DiDi taxi like this. Oh, someone picked up the order, you see, the plate number is QS189, and we can check its route in real time.

Smith: Ah, it is super convenient.

Oven: That's right. It is really convenient and cost-effective in China. The car is coming, let me get you in the car.

Smith: OK, many thanks to you.

Oven: Wish you have a good trip, sir! Good-bye.

Smith: Bye-bye.

Situational dialogue 3

Context: Shirley picked up a T-shirt in room 8018. She handed it to the receptionist Joyce.

Tasks:

1. Discuss with your group members about how to deal with the items that guests forgot to take away.

2. Try to rehearse this dialogue.

Shirley: Hello, Joyce. I picked up a T-shirt in room 8018 this morning. Would you please contact the guest?

Joyce: Certainly. Thank you so much.

...

Joyce: Good afternoon, Mr. Smith. This is receptionist Joyce from the hotel.

Smith: Good afternoon.

Joyce: Our housekeeper found a T-shirt in your room. Have you lost a T-shirt?

Smith: Oh, god. It is mine. Is there a white cat on the T-shirt?

Joyce: Yes. A white cat. How would you like to have it back?

Smith: Could you please send it to you through the express service?

Joyce: Sure, we have your telephone and address in the system. May I confirm with you for the information? Your telephone number is 13456789000, your address is No.208 Road, Jingde

Town, Jiangxi province. Is that right?

Smith: Yes. Thank you so much.

Joyce: You are welcome. Have a nice journey! Good-bye.

Smith: Good-bye.

Part IV Vocabulary & Notes

Textbook	Word stress	Translation
iconic	i-CO-nic	符号的；图标的；偶像的
monogram	MO-no-gram	字母组合
fuse	FUSE	熔化；融合
bernache	ber-NA-che	Accor 的图标（现指"大雁"）
emblem	EM-blem	象征；标记；典型；用象征表示
infinite	IN-fi-nite	无限的；无穷的；许许多多的
deliver	de-LI-ver	发表；递送；投递；传送
exceptional	ex-CEP-tion-al	优越的；杰出的；独特的
passion	PASSION	激情；热情；热心；爱好；热恋
innovation	in-no-VA-tion	改革；创新；新观念
commitment	com-MIT-ment	承诺；委任；承担义务
sustainability	sus-tai-na-BI-li-ty	持续性；能维持性；永续性
holistic	ho-LIS-tic	全盘的；整体的
ecosystem	ECO-sys-tem	生态系统
consumer	con-SU-mer	消费者；顾客
luxury	LUX-u-ry	奢侈；豪华；奢侈品；享受
aparthotel	a-PART-ho-tel	公寓式酒店
thalasso	tha-LA-sso	水疗酒店
compose	com-POSE	组成；构成；调解
launch	LAUNCH	发射；开展；投入；着手进行
receipt	re-CEIPT	收据；收入
short	SHORT	短裤；缺乏；还差…
concierge	con-ci-ERGE	礼宾；礼宾处
bind	BIND	约束；装订；捆绑

Notes

1. advanced deposit 预付押金
2. credit card 信用卡
3. emergency contact person 紧急联系人
4. in real time 实时的
5. apply for 申请

阅读译文

雅高酒店集团

雅高集团标志性的字母"A"是"集团卓越"的标志,融合了大雁(Bernache)这一雅高有着历史意义的集团徽标。

热忱待客的艺术无边界。它不局限于建筑的高墙内,而是闪耀在每个细节之中。雅高大胆地重新定义了酒店行业:它不仅仅意味着一栋建筑、一项服务,无论客人下榻酒店是为了生活、工作或是娱乐,雅高集团更是联系彼此的无数个时刻。雅高正在全力塑造这样一种未来:旅行解锁了生活的无限可能;强大的品牌带去非凡的体验与价值,优质服务与热情则送上贴心的人文关怀;锐意创新不断拓展服务疆域,可持续发展的承诺守护着大家的共同家园。这就是雅高打造以消费者为中心的完整产业生态,并在创新服务与解决方案方面不断创新,以孜孜不倦推动发展的动力。未来属于精心规划未来之人,而雅高正致力于成为这样的先锋,率先将客人带入美好的未来。

雅高集团旗下的50个品牌酒店(其中38个品牌囊括了奢华至经济型的各种档位)欢迎客人入住全球100个国家的4800多家酒店(704,000间客房),尽享难忘的酒店体验。从奢华型到经济型酒店,从公寓式酒店到水疗酒店,在众多目的地中尽享最优选择,实现梦想,重新发现全球旅游的意义。迄今为止,大约有280,000名员工供职于雅高酒店集团旗下各品牌。

雅高酒店集团发展历程:

1967年,第一家诺富特酒店在法国里尔开业;
1974年,第一家宜必思酒店在法国波尔多开业;
1975年,并购美居品牌;
1980年,收购索菲特品牌;
1984年,进入中国市场,第一家诺富特酒店开业;
1990年,收购美国Motel 6和Lenotre品牌;
2001年,宜必思品牌进入中国;
2007年,重塑铂尔曼品牌;
2008年,创建美憬阁品牌;
2012年,达成雅高酒店集团亚太区500家酒店里程碑;
2013年,全球第100家诺富特酒店在普吉岛开业;
2014年,雅高酒店集团收购诗铂品牌;
2015年,与华住集团开展战略合作;
2016年,收购奢华私人住宅租赁市场中的全球领先品牌Onefinestay,与悦榕集团达成战略合作;
2017年,法国前总统萨科齐加入雅高酒店集团主管国际战略委员会,收购Rixos品牌;
2018年,收购瑞享Movenpick等品牌;
2019年,提出全新集团品牌标识与生活方式忠诚计划。

Part V Discussion

How do you think of the guests' impression of the hotel? And how to make good impression to your guests?

Part VI Writing

According to what you have learned in this unit, try to write a letter of thanks to your guests.

Module 5
Airport Service

Unit 14 | Seeing-off service

Learning objectives

1. Know the procedure of seeing off the tourists.
2. Master the useful expression of seeing off.
3. Know how to help the agents before them get on the plane and leave.

Part I Warming up

Here are three scenes of departure at the airport. Imagine a possible conversation between a tour guide and a guest.

"I've decided to live in the present and not spend my life regretting the past or dreading the future."

（我决定活在当下，不浪费光阴去为过去后悔或为未来担忧。）

——Unknown

Part II Reading

Seeing People Off

——Max Beerbohm

I am not good at it. To do it well seems to me one of the most difficult things in the world, and probably seems so to you, too.

To see a friend off from Waterloo to Vauxhall were easy enough. But we are never called on to perform that small feat. It is only when a friend is going on a longish journey, and will be absent for a longish time, that we turn up at the railway station. The dearer the friend, and the longer the journey, and the longer the likely absence, the earlier do we turn up, and the more lamentably do we fail. Our failure is in exact ratio to the seriousness of the occasion, and to the depth of our feeling.

In a room or even on a door step, we can make the farewell quite worthily. We can express in our faces the genuine sorrow we feel. Nor do words fail us. There is no awkwardness, no restraint on either side. The thread of our intimacy has not been snapped. The leave-taking is an ideal one. Why no, then leave the leave-taking at that? Always, departing friends implore us not to bother to come to the railway station next morning. Always, we are deaf to these entreaties, knowing them to be not quite sincere. The departing friends would think it very odd of us if we took them at their word. Besides, they really do want to see us again. And that wish is heartily reciprocated. We duly turn up. And then, oh then, what a gulf yawns! We stretch our arms vainly across it. We have utterly lost touch. We have nothing at all to say. We gaze at each other as dumb animals gaze at human beings. We make conversation -- and such conversation! We know that these friends are the friends from whom we parted overnight. They know that we have not altered. Yet, on the surface, everything is different; and the tension is such that we only long for the guard to blow his whistle and put an end to the farce.

On a cold grey morning of last week I duly turned up at Euston, to see off an old friend who was starting for America. Overnight, we had given him a farewell dinner, in which sadness was well mingled with festivity. Years probably would elapse before his return. Some of us might never see him again. Not ignoring the shadow of the future, we gaily celebrated the past. We were as thankful to have known our guest as we were grieved to lose him; and both these emotions were made manifest. It was a perfect farewell.

And now, here we were, stiff and self-conscious on the platform; and framed in the window of the railway-carriage was the face of our friend; but it was as the face of a stranger -- a stranger anxious to please, an appealing stranger, an awkward stranger. Have you got everything? Asked one of us, breaking a silence. Yes, everything, said our friend, with a pleasant nod. "Everything, " he repeated, with the emphasis of an empty brain. "You'll be able to lunch on the train, " said I, though the prophecy had already been made more than once. "Oh, yes," he said with conviction. He added that the train went straight through to Liverpool. This fact seemed to strike us as rather odd, we exchanged glances. "Doesn't it stop at Crewe？" Asked one of us. "No," said our friend, briefly. He seemed almost disagreeable. There was a long pause. One of us, with a nod and a forced smile at the traveler, said "Well！" The nod, the smile and the unmeaning monosyllable were returned conscientiously. Another pause was broken by one of us with a fit of coughing. It was an obviously assumed fit, but it served to pass the time. The bustle of the platform was unabated. There was no sign of the train's departure. Release--ours, and our friend's, -- was not yet.

My wandering eye alighted on a rather portly middle-aged man who was talking earnestly from the platform to a young lady at the next window but one to ours. His fine profile was vaguely familiar to me. The young lady was evidently American, and he was evidently English; otherwise I should have guessed from his impressive air that he was her father. I wished I could hear what he was saying. I was sure he was giving the very best advice; and the strong tenderness of his gaze was really beautiful. He seemed magnetic, as he poured out his final injunctions. I could feel something of his magnetism even where I stood. And the magnetism like the profile, was vaguely familiar to me. Where had I experienced it？

In a flash I remembered. The man was Hubert Le Ros. But how changed since last I saw him！ That was seven or eight years ago, in the Strand. He was then as usual out of an engagement, and borrowed half a crown. It seemed a privilege to lend anything to him. He was always magnetic. And why his magnetism had never made him successful on the London stage was always a mystery to me. He was an excellent actor, and a man of sober habit. But, like many others of his kind, Hubert Le Ros（I do not, of course, give the actual name by which he was known）drifted speedily away into the provinces；and I, like everyone else, ceased to remember him.

It was strange to see him, after all these years, here on the platform of Euston, looking so prosperous and solid. It was not only the flesh that he had put on, but also the clothes, that made him hard to recognize. In the old days, an imitation fur coat had seemed to be as integral a part of him as were his ill-shorn lantern jaws. But now his costume was a model of rich and somber moderation, drawing, not calling attention to itself. He looked like a banker. Anyone would have been proud to be seen off by him.

"Stand back, please!" The train was about to start, and I waved farewell to my friend. Le Ros did not stand back. He stood clasping in both hands the hands of the young American. "Stand back, sir, please!" He obeyed, but quickly darted forward again to whisper some final word. I think there were tears in her eyes. There certainly were tears in his when, at length, having watched the train out of sight, he turned round. He seemed, nevertheless, delighted to see me. He asked me where I had been hiding all these years; and simultaneously repaid me the half-crown as though it had been borrowed yesterday. He linked his arm in mine, and walked with me slowly along the platform, saying with what pleasure he read my dramatic criticisms every Saturday.

After reading, please answer the questions below:

1. What's the feeling of "me", when "I" see "my" friends off on the platform?
2. Why did "I" think Hubert Le Ros has changed a lot now compared to the past?
3. What did Hubert Le Ros think that I lack when "I" see someone off?
4. In your opinion, what did you think the most important matter when you attempt to see off a friend?

Part III Listening

Listen to *dialogues* and finish the tasks.

Situational dialogue 1

*Context: On the last day of the trip, national guide **Shirley** leads the guests to take the coach to Shuangliu International Airport to check in. Before departure, **Shirley** reminds the guests on the coach to check whether they have their boarding passes and personal belongings with them.*

Task: answer the questions below.

1. When will they arrive at the airport according to the schedule?
2. At the restaurant at the airport, what does the tour guide recommend to the guests?
3. What were in the envelope that the tour guide handed out to the guests before they went back to their room last night?
4. To get on the plane, what should guests take with? Try to rehearse this dialogue.

Shirley: All right, everybody got on? Please have a look again if your family and friends get on the bus, we will leave soon.

Andy: All on board.

Shirley: OK, thanks. Today, we are about to end our week-long pleasant trip and go to Chengdu Shuangliu International Airport to take Sichuan Airlines flight U3888 to New York at 2:45 p.m. It's 8:50 a.m. now, we will leave in 10 minutes and arrive at terminal T1 of Shuangliu International Airport in 1 hour. My driver, Mr Liu and I will accompany you till the end of this journey.

Bain: Where are we going to have lunch?

Shirley: In order to ensure that everyone has enough time to check-in, the envelope that I handed out to you before you went back to your room last night has the discount coupons for the duty-free shop at the airport and the meal vouchers at the terminal. After check-in, you can eat at the designated restaurant on the voucher.

Bain: Wow, there is Sichuan Style Wonton. Is it the Sichuan Style Wonton that we had the day before yesterday?

Shirley: Yes, they are chain stores. I recommend Sichuan Style Wonton and Sichuan noodles with chili sauce at this restaurant at the airport, which I believe will make your last meal memorable. Before the coach starts, please make sure you have your passport, boarding pass, discount coupons and meal vouchers.

Eric: Oh, god. My passport isn't in my bag. I think I put it in the suitcase.

Shirley: OK, I'll tell the driver, Mr. Liu to open the luggage compartment. Come with me and Let's check it.

Eric: thanks. I really hope I put it in the suitcase.

Shirley: It should be there; you all used your passport before we went back to our room yesterday. Before I left this morning, I asked the front desk of the hotel to contact the guest room and found no lost items in everyone's room. Is there anyone else who needs to come down to get the ID?

Daniel: Can I get my power bank?

Shirley: Oh, sure. Please also take all kinds of electronic products along with you, including your laptop. They cannot be put in the checked-in luggage.

Eric: Thank god, it's in my suitcase.

Shirley: It is good that it is found. OK, it's precisely nine o'clock, we are leaving on time. Let's go.

Situational dialogue 2

Context: On the way to the airport, national guide **Shirley** *leads the guests to summarize the trip.*

Tasks: answer the questions below.

1. What is the next destination of the group?
2. Where did the group visit in Chengdu?
3. In memory of the great strategist and politician Zhuge liang, which historical site of Chengdu can we choose according to the text?
4. Where did the flower exhibition launch?

Shirley: Our week-long trip to Sichuan is coming to an end. Thank you for your support and company along the way. Sincerely, I believe we have left beautiful memories for each other.

With the time goes quickly, we visit Chengdu is drawing to a close. The tourist's new destination is Xian. This afternoon you will be leaving Chengdu for Xian by plane. When you arrive at Shuangliu Airport, I shall be very busy with handing the boarding pass and taking care of your luggage. So, I could hardly have time to say goodbye to everyone. So, let me take this opportunity to say something about our wonderful trip.

When we arrive at the Chengdu, we are surprised in progress and prosperity. When we visited the Wuhou Temple, nobody failed to experience Romance of the Three Kingdoms history and know one of the most famous person Zhuge Liang. When we walked leisurely in Sansheng flower town, we feel exciting to appreciate all kind of flowers in the flower exhibition.

First of all, thanks for your understanding and cooperation you have given us in two days. You have been forgiving and understand, offer us suggestions on how to solve the problem when I was making mistakes. I want to say in my heart that you are the best group we've ever.

Parting is such sweet sorrow. We believe that Chinese word said "A bosom friend afar brings a distant land near." We are friend forever. We turn on the telephone for 24 hours to serve you. Welcome to call me. Ha!!! I hope to see you again in the future and to be your guide again.

At last, I can't talk the something best, but whenever and wherever, best wishes for you. Everything goes well! Being in good health! Fortune star shine high! May all you wishe would come true! Wish you prosperity! And so on.

Once again, thank you for cooperation and support.

Situational dialogue 3

The national guide **Shirley** *is seeing off the tourists at the airport.*

Task: answers questions below

1. What should Shirley remind the tourists?
2. What will the porter do?
3. What identification do we need when checking in?
4. Which check-in counters can be used by the tourists?
5. When will Shirley leave the airport?

Shirley: Well, here we are at the airport. All present and correct!

Andy: Yes, and on time!

Shirley: I'll go and get some porters. Please remind the tourists not to leave anything behind, and take care of their valuables.

Andy: OK, thank you.

(A few minutes later)

Shirley: I'm back. The porters will take the luggage so we can make our way straight to the check-in counters—B3 to B8.

Andy: Thanks a lot! I'll ask everyone to identify their luggage.

Shirley: OK, fine. Please remind all tourists to keep their ID cards in their hands when waiting in line for check-in.

Andy: OK. Will you wait until we have checked in, just in case there are any problems?

Shirley: Yes, of course. I'll be here until you have cleared security.

Andy: Thank you. I'm sure everything will be fine but just in case!

Shirley: No problem. And I hope you have a good flight and a safe journey home. Please keep in touch and if I can do anything for you, please let me know.

Andy: Thank you. You are so nice.

Part IV Vocabulary

Textbook	Word stress	Translation
absent	AB-sent	缺席；缺少；心不在焉的
lamentably	LA-men-ta-bly	哀伤地；不幸地；拙劣地
seriousness	SE-rious-ness	严重；认真；严肃
occasion	oc-CA-sion	时机；造成；导致
depth	DEPTH	深厚；诚挚；强烈
awkwardness	AW-kward-ness	笨拙；粗劣；难为情；尴尬
entreaty	en-TREA-ty	恳求；乞求
conversation	con-ver-SA-tion	(非正式) 交谈，谈话
festivity	fes-TI-vi-ty	庆祝活动；欢庆；欢乐
emphasis	EM-pha-sis	强调；重视；重要性
conscientiously	con-sci-EN-tious-ly	一丝不苟地
assume	as-SUME	假定；认为；承担 (责任)
departure	de-PAR-ture	离开；起程；出发
familiar	fa-MI-liar	熟悉的；常见到的；常客
injunction	in-JUNC-tion	警告；指令；命令
magnetism	MAG-ne-tism	吸引力；魅力
prosperous	PRO-spe-rous	繁荣的；成功的；兴旺的
accompany	ac-COM-pany	陪同；陪伴；伴随
ensure	en-SURE	保证；担保；确保
memorable	ME-mo-rable	值得纪念的；难忘的
aftertaste	AF-ter-taste	余味；苦味
compartment	com-PART-ment	隔间；隔层
electronic	e-lec-TRO-nic	电子的；电子设备的
destination	des-ti-NA-tion	目的地；终点
appreciate	ap-PRE-ci-ate	欣赏；赏识；重视
exhibition	ex-hi-BI-tion	展示；表示；表演
explain	ex-PLAIN	解释；说明

Textbook	Word stress	Translation
location	lo-CA-tion	地方；地点；位置
moisturizing spray	mois-tu-RI-zing spray	喷雾
cream	CREAM	面霜
perfume	per-FUME	香水
duty-free shop	DU-ty-free shop	免税店
cosmetics	cos-ME-tics	化妆品；美容品
transparent	trans-PA-rent	透明的
plastic	PLAS-tic	塑料
immediately	im-ME-di-a-tely	立即；马上

阅读译文

送行

我不会送行。它可是我所认为的世上最难做好的事情之一。对此，你大概也心有同感。

送一位朋友从滑铁卢去沃克斯豪尔可以说是一件相当简单的事。但你从来就接不到这种轻松活儿。我们只有当朋友要远行，离去的时间又比较长久时，才被召唤亲赴车站送行。朋友交情越好，送的路程越远，朋友离去的时间越长，我们就越早到达车站，相应地，我们遭遇的失败也就越为惨烈。这种失败的程度恰恰与场合的正式以及感情的深厚程度成正比。

屋内话别已十分体面，甚至在门前台阶也不错。我们脸上的表情书写着真切的忧伤，言语里透出恋恋不舍之情，主客双方不觉尴尬或拘谨，亲密友谊更是丝毫无损。如此的送别真可谓完美。可我们怎么就不懂到了这种程度就应该罢休呢？通常情况下，即将远行的友人们总是恳求我们次日早晨不要再赶到车站。但我们知道那不一定是真心话，便也就不听信那些劝说的话，还是奔向车站。假若真的听信了朋友们的话，并且照着做了，他们说不定心里还会责怪呢。何况，他们也确实希望能和我们再见上一面。于是我们也就按时到达，真诚地去回应朋友的愿望。但结果却，结果却，陡然生出一道鸿沟！我们伸手，可怎么也无法超越，谁也够不着谁。我们哑口无言，像愚笨的动物痴望人类一样面面相觑。我们"找些话题来说"——但哪里有什么话好说的！大家都心知肚明，离别之景昨夜就已上演了一遍。人还是昨晚的那些人，但从表面上看，所有的又都变了。气氛是如此紧张，我们都盼望着列车员赶紧鸣笛，及早结束这场闹剧。

上周一个冷清阴沉的早晨，我准点赶到奥斯顿送一位去美国的朋友。

头一天晚上，我们已经摆设筵席为他饯行，席间分手的离情和聚会的喜庆把握得恰到好处。他这一去可能就是多年，席上有些人恐怕今世也难得再见。虽然说不上完全不受未来所投下的阴影的影响，可我们还是兴高采烈，畅叙了往日情谊。我们既为认识这位朋友而感谢命运，同时又因他的行将离别而遗憾不已。此两种情怀欣然体现，昨晚的离别真是完美！

可现在呢，我们在站台上，行为僵硬，极不自然，友人的面孔嵌在车厢窗框中，却宛然属于一个陌生人——一个急于讨人欢心的陌生人，一个情意真切但却举止笨拙的陌生人。"东西都带齐了吧？"送行的人中有一个打破了沉默。"对，都带齐了。"我们的朋友愉快地点了点头，答道"都齐了。"紧接着的这次再重复更加明显地暴露出此刻他头脑的空空如也。"那你得在火车上吃午饭了"我说道，尽管这个预言远非是第一次被提出。"啊，是的。"他用确定的语气回答，然后又告诉大家，列车将中途不停直达利物浦。这句新加上的话似乎就带来了惊讶。我们彼此对视。"在克鲁也不停吗？"一个人问道。"不停"朋友回答得简短甚至都有些不悦了。较长一段时间的停顿过后，有个人对我们的朋友回了句"好"，与此同时还点着头，做强颜欢笑状。于是，车外每个人都那般点头，吐出那个莫名其妙的单音词"好"，以表谢意。沉默再次接踵而至，多亏我们中的一位干咳了几声打破这沉闷的寂静——那咳嗽当然是假装出来的，但它们却恰到好处地拖延了时间。列车似乎没有立即出发的迹象，站台上还是乱哄哄的。关于解除送别紧张的气氛——无论是送客的，还是被送的——这个时刻还没有到来。

我的目光四处游弋，移到一个中年人身上的时候眼前突然一亮，他体格颇为健壮，站在站台上，正同我们旁边第三个窗口里的一名年轻女郎亲切话别。他良好的体型于我似乎并不陌生。那女郎显然是个美国人，而他英国人的特征也十分明显。如果不注意这点，单从他娓娓而谈的神态判断，我定会把他们当成一对父女。我热切地想听到他说话的内容，十分确定他此时正提供着最宝贵的建议；而他又是那般温柔地凝视着他的倾听者，真是活脱脱的一个美男子。末了，他又叮咛几句，更是魅力慑人了，连站在那么远之外的我都能感受到。而这魅力，就好比他的身材，隐隐约约为我所熟悉。但是，我在哪儿见到过呢？

我猛地想起来了。他是休伯特·勒·罗斯。可是，比起最后一次见面，他发生了多大的改变呀！那都是七八年前在滨河路的事了。当时他正失业（失业对他而言再正常不过了），来找我借半克朗。他是如此魅力非凡，借他点儿东西都能让人受宠若惊。但凭着那样的魅力，他竟一直没在伦敦舞台红起来，其中道理我是猜不透的。他滴酒不沾，是一个优秀的演员。可他也游走到外地了，像其他许许多多休伯特·勒·罗斯一样（当然，我在这所写下的并非他的真名）。于是我也就像别人一样，没过多少时日就把他遗忘了。

时光流逝，在奥斯顿的站台上再度见到他真有些陌生感，尤其是他现在如此地阔气殷实。把他给认出来可真不容易，其一是几乎令他面目全非发福了的身材，其二更是他今非昔比的衣着。多年前，他两颊瘦瘪，胡子拉碴，一件人造毛皮大衣是唯一能让他抛头露面的皮囊。但如今，他的穿戴典型地透出富贵而内敛的风格。他无须去引人注目，人们自然而然就会被他所吸引。有他这样一位具备银行家气质的人前来送行，被送的人都会甚感荣幸。

"请后退，请后退！"列车就要开了，我也挥手向朋友告别。可勒·罗斯并没有动，依旧站在那儿握着那美国女郎的双手。"请后退，先生！"他照做了，但立即又冲了回去，上前耳语了最后一句珍重之辞。我猜，当时女郎一定泪眼汪汪了吧。而最终当他目送列车驶出视线，转过身时，他眼里也噙满了泪。不过，见到我时他还是表现得很高兴。他一边询问这些年来我都隐匿在什么地方，一边还给我那半克朗，仿佛这钱他昨天才刚刚借去。他说每星期六我发表的那些剧评是如何赏心悦目，同时还把我的手挽起，沿着站台一路缓缓地走。

Part V Discussion

1. What did you learn from this unit?

2. If you are the tour guide in Chengdu, what specialties and spots of Chengdu will you recommend to your guests?

3. In your eye, what are the useful and indispensable words when you decide to see off a friend or an agent separately?

Part VI Writing

According to this unit, and then try your hand at writing a farewell speech.

Unit 15 | Baggage Check-in

Learning objectives

1. Knowing about the procedure of check-in at the airport.
2. Master the useful expressions about check-in.
3. Know how to deal with the emergency situation like losing the passport and facing the delayed flight and so on.

Part I Warming up

Collect all the airport signs you know and remember their English expressions.

"There are thousands of ways if you wish and tons of reasons if you refuse."（倘若心中所愿，道路千千条；倘若心中有碍，理由万万种。）

——Unknown

Part II Reading

How much do you know about the airport?

Chengdu Shuangliu International Airport, located in the hometown of Pandas -- Chengdu, Sichuan Province, is the fourth largest aviation hub in Mainland China and is speeding up the construction of an international aviation hub with "connectivity and global reach" in western China.Chengdu Shuangliu International Airport is located in the west of Shuangliu County, southwest of Chengdu, 16.825 km away from downtown Chengdu.The entire airport covers an area of 14,106 acres.Chengdu Shuangliu International Airport is one of the 50 busiest airports in the world. It is the center of air passenger and cargo distribution in inland southwest China, and the most important civil aviation administrative center in southwest China.

Shuangliu Airport enjoys the titles of "National Health Airport", "National Civilized Airport", "National Customer satisfaction Enterprise", etc. Since its establishment, it has been one of the top ten busiest airports in China, and has maintained a record of zero safety accidents. Chengdu Shuangliu International Airport has two terminals with a total area of 500,000 square meters and an annual passenger throughput of 50 million passengers.

Terminal 1 is for international flights and Sichuan Airlines import and export flights. Terminal 1 has three parallel corridors (A, B and C), one fast passageway for domestic and foreign passengers, and is equipped with port system, building automation system, etc.In 2004, the area of the international terminal building reached 39,000 square meters.

Terminal 2 provides check-in services for domestic flights other than Sichuan Airlines. Terminal 2 is located next to the original feeder terminal.The terminal's second building covers an area of 350,000 square meters. The airport is a steel truss structure, and its bamboo leaves show the local characteristics of Sichuan.Terminal 2 has added four corridors -- D, E, F and G -- to the third in Terminal 1. Inside the terminal sets up six check-in islands, 120 security channels at check-in counters, more than 170 elevators, escalators and moving walks, and an automatic baggage sorting system. China international aviation also has its first class and business class passenger exclusive service area in Terminal 2, offering dining, sleeping, showers and other services.

On December 12, 2012, throughput of Shuangliu Airport has more than 30 million people. Shuangliu Airport is the fifth airport in China after Beijing Capital International Airport, Guangzhou Baiyun International Airport, Shanghai Pudong Airport and Shanghai Hongqiao Airport, the only one in the Midwest for the airport passenger throughput of more than 30 million people. In 2012, there were 31.59 million passengers.In 2013, the number of passengers reached

33.4 million, ranking fifth in China.

Chengdu Shuangliu International Airport will play an increasingly prominent role as the hub airport in western China. I wish the airport will have a more beautiful environment, better services and more modern facilities, and become China's western airport gate facing the world.

After reading, please answer the questions below:
1. What is the exact location of Shuangliu airport?
2. What honors have Shuangliu airport gotten so far?
3. What functions do Terminal 1 and Terminal 2 have respectively?
4. If you are an employee of Shuangliu airport, what suggestions will you give to improve the airport, and why?

Part III Listening

Listen to *dialogues* and finish the tasks.

Situational dialogue 1

Context: The ground agent at the Information Desk **Cindy** is helping the guest **Eric** who checks in at the airport for the first time.

Task: answer the questions below.
1. Where should Eric check in?
2. What does the guest need when getting on the plane?
3. What is the free checked baggage allowance?

Cindy: Hello, what can I do for you?

Eric: Oh, hello. I would like to check in, but this is my first time to the airport. I'm not sure what to do?

Cindy: Where are you going, sir?

Eric: London.

Cindy : OK, sir, firstly you need to print your boarding pass and check-in your luggage at F, just turn right, you can go to the counter with your passport to get your boarding pass and check-in.

Eric: OK, thank you.

Cindy: You are welcome. Is there anything else I can do for you?

Eric: Yes, I want to know the free allowance for luggage.

Cindy: The Sichuan Airline's free checked baggage allowance: 20kg for economy class,

30 kg for business class.

Eric: Can I take my small suitcase on the plane?

Cindy: Yes, you can take it with you for security check. After that, you can go to K17 gate according to the instructions and wait for boarding. Please keep your passport and boarding pass. If you would like to buy something at duty-free stores, just show your passport and boarding pass to the clerk.

Eric: OK. Thank you very much.

Cindy: It's my pleasure. I hope you enjoy your flight.

Situational dialogue 2

Context: The airport official **Frank** is helping the guest **Eric** to check in. But **Eric** lost his passport.

Tasks: answer the questions below.

1. What happened to the passenger?
2. Did Eric miss the flight?
3. What should we do if we lost our passport when check-in?

Frank: Hello, May I help you?

Eric: I want to check in. I have 2 big suitcases. I guess it overweight.

Frank: Please put your suitcases on the scale and show me your passport.

Eric: Please wait for a moment. Sorry, I can't find my passport.

Frank: May I have a look at your boarding information? Well, don' worry, it's 11:00 in the morning and there's plenty of time. You can go to the lost-and-found office at 2nd floor, perhaps they can help you.

  (20 minutes later)

Eric: I'm so sorry. I didn't find my passport. But I have a driver's license. Is it OK?

Frank: That's great. I will contact the British Embassy in Chengdu and the Entry-exit Administration Bureau at the airport to confirm your identity information and report the loss of your passport.

Eric: OK, really thank you. (*Eric found his passport in his pocket*...) Oh, thank goodness, I seem to have found my passport.

Frank: That's too good. It will be really troublesome to go through the embassy and the entry-exit Administration Bureau if it is not found.

Eric: Yes, thanks a lot. Here you are.

Frank: You are welcome. Sir, your luggage is overweight by 7kg, you need to pay 140 yuan more in cash.

Eric: OK, here you are.

Frank: Which seat do you prefer, a window seat or an aisle seat?

Eric: Window seat, please.

Frank: This is your boarding pass and passport. Wish you a pleasant flight.

Situational dialogue 3

*Context: The Flight U8887, which was supposed to leave Chengdu Shuangliu Airport at 11:20 a.m., was delayed by heavy rain for about 4 hours. There is no news of any departure from Shuangliu Airport. The guest **Eric** was very angry about it, and the staff **Beta** is dealing with the problem.*

Task: answer the questions below.
1. Why is the flight delayed?
2. How long did the guest wait for?
3. Summary the procedure of helping the delayed guests.

Eric: Hello, when will the flight U8887 take off? We've been waiting here for almost four hours.

Beta: I'm terribly sorry. All flights to London are now delayed because of the weather.

Eric: But it's clear outside the airport now.

Beta: Yes, the weather here is very good, but there has been a sudden rainstorm near London Airport since this morning. In order to ensure the safe landing, we and the local airport are keeping an eye on the local weather changes.

Eric: But we have been waiting for 4 hours.

Beta: I'm sorry to have kept you waiting so long. But the London Weather Bureau said there is a rare rainstorm today with thunderstorms. All flights are grounded at London Airport. Based on the current situation, it is difficult to guarantee a safe landing if we take off now.

Eric: I'm really anxious. It is my daughter's birthday and I want to go back to accompany her as soon as possible.

Beta: I can understand your feelings, but for the safety of you and guests of the whole plane, we cannot make the decision to take off until the security information is transmitted back. I'm really sorry.

Eric: I'm really unlucky. This is my first time to your airport.

Beta: Sorry for the extreme inconvenience.London Airport updates the local weather information every half an hour.We will inform the guests as soon as possible as soon as the instruction for take off is sent back.

Eric: What if we can't take off today?

Beta: We have contacted the airport hotel. If we cannot take off today, we will arrange free check-in stay for every guest flying to London. Meals are provided tonight and before departure.

Eric: This is really embarrassing. Well, please let me know as soon as you get the message to take off.

Beta: OK, apologize again.

Module 5 Airport Service 125

Part IV   Vocabulary

Textbook	Word stress	Translation
midwest	mid-WEST	中西部
aviation	a-vi-A-tion	航空
passenger	PA-ssen-ger	乘客
cargo	CAR-go	（由船或飞机装载的）货物
distribution	dis-tri-BU-tion	（商品）运销
headquarters	HEAD-quar-ters	总部；总公司；大本营
enterprise	EN-ter-prise	公司；企业；事业单位
establishment	e-STA-blish-ment	机构；大型组织
terminal	TER-mi-nal	航站楼
domestic flight	do-MES-tic flight	国内航班
characteristic	cha-rac-te-RIS-tic	典型的；独特的；特有的
Lhasa	LHA-sa	拉萨
annual cumulative	AN-nual cu-mu-la-tive	年复一年的积累
environment	en-VI-ron-ment	环境
vacant	VA-cant	空着的；未被占用的
security check	se-CU-ri-ty check	安检
assure	as-SURE	自信的；有把握的
prohibit	pro-HI-bit	禁止
conveyor belt	con-VE-yor belt	传送带
document	DO-cu-ment	文件夹
electronics	e-lec-TRO-nics	电子产品
toiletry	TOI-le-try	化妆用具；化妆品
medication	me-di-CA-tion	药物
overweight	o-ver-WEIGHT	超重
measure	MEA-sure	测量
ceramic	ce-RA-mic	陶瓷
dozen bag	DO-zen bag	登机箱（12寸）
grocery	GRO-ce-ry	杂货店
valid identification	va-lid i-den-ti-fi-CA-tion	身份证明
driver's license	DRI-ver's li-cense	驾照
Embassy	EM-ba-ssy	大使馆
Entry-exit Administration Bureau		出入境管理局

阅读译文

你对机场了解有多少

成都双流国际机场位于"熊猫故乡"——四川成都,是中国大陆第四大航空枢纽,即正加快建设中国西部"互联互通、辐射全球"的国际航空枢纽。成都双流国际机场坐落于成都西南部双流县的西面,距离成都市中心16.825公里。整个机场占地面积为14106英亩。成都双流国际机场是世界上最繁忙的50个机场之一,是中国内陆西南地区航空旅客和货运的集散中心,同时也是西南地区最重要的民航行政中心。

双流机场享有"国家卫生机场""国家文明机场""国家用户满意企业"等称号,自成立以来一直是中国十大最繁忙机场之一,并保持着零安全事故的记录。成都双流国际机场有两个航站楼,总面积50万平方米,年旅客吞吐量可达5000万人次。

1号航站楼供国际航班和四川航空公司的进出口航班使用。1号航站楼有三条平行指廊(A、B、C指廊),一条供国内外旅客使用的快捷通道,并设有港口系统、楼宇自动化系统等。2004年,国际候机楼的面积达到3.9万平方米。

2号航站楼为四川航空以外的国内航班提供值机服务。2号航站楼坐落于原来的支线航站楼旁。航站楼的第二栋建筑占地35万平方米,机场为钢桁架结构,竹叶呈现了四川的地方特色。2号航站楼在1号航站楼三个指廊的基础上增加了D、E、F、G四个指廊。航站楼内设有6个值机岛、120个人工值机柜台安检通道,170多部电梯、自动扶梯和自动人行道,并配置了行李自动分拣系统。中国国际航空还在二号航站楼设有头等舱和公务舱旅客专属服务区,提供餐饮、睡眠、淋浴和其他服务。

2012年12月12日,双流机场年吞吐量已超过3000万人次,成为继北京首都国际机场、广州白云国际机场、上海浦东机场、上海虹桥机场之后中国第五个、中西部唯一一个全年客运吞吐量超过3000万人次的机场。2012年,旅客人数为3159万人次。2013年,旅客总数达到3340万人次,居全国第五位。

成都双流国际机场作为中国西部枢纽机场的功能和地位将日益凸显,祝愿机场环境更加优美,服务更加完善周到,设施更加现代化,成为中国面向世界的西部空港大门。

Part V Discussion

1. What did you learn from this unit?
2. Compare the procedure of check-in with that of helping the agent who lost his passport.

3. Suppose you are a steward; you meet a passenger who is particular and impatient. How will you do when you are serving the passenger?

Part VI Writing

According to this unit, try to write a script about ground service and play it with your partners.

Unit 16 | Duty-free Shopping

Learning objectives

1. Know about duty-free shops and items.
2. Master the useful words and expressions about duty-free shopping.
3. Know how to provide duty-free sale service.

Part I | Warming up

1. Can you list the world's top 10 airport duty-free stores with their corresponding country?

（1）Dubai International Airport Duty Free　　　　　　　　　　　（　）
（2）Sydney International Airport Duty Free　　　　　　　　　　　（　）
（3）Tokyo Haneda International Airport Duty Free　　　　　　　　（　）
（4）New York Kennedy International Airport Duty Free　　　　　　（　）
（5）Seoul Incheon International Airport Duty Free　　　　　　　　（　）
（6）Hong Kong Chek lap kok International Airport Duty Free　　　（　）
（7）Rome's Fiumicino International Airport Duty Free　　　　　　（　）
（8）Charles DE Gaulle International Airport Duty Free　　　　　　（　）
（9）Singapore's Changi International Airport Duty Free　　　　　 （　）
（10）Beijing Capital International Airport Duty Free　　　　　　　（　）

2. Can you name the following duty-free items?

cigarettes　　confectionery　　cosmetics　　electronic goods　　bags
jewelry　　skincare products　　watches　　perfumes

_____　　_____　　_____

"It can be said that DFS is a luxury department store suitable for different travelers around the world"

（可以说DFS是一家适合世界各地不同游客的奢侈品百货公司）

DFS Senior vice President,
global marketing and promotion
——Winnie Park

Part II Reading

The World's Largest Duty-Free Shop Haitang Bay Duty-Free Shopping Center

Sanya Haitang Bay duty-free shopping center, with a total construction area of about 120,000 square meters and a commercial area of 72,000 square meters, is the largest single duty-free shop in the world. The vast shopping center not only contains a variety of formats, but also has more functional experience. Louis Vuitton, Prada, Giorgio Armani and many other international top brands have settled in the city. Besides, it also brings five functional zones of various commodities of national characteristics, Hainan specialties, outdoor sports, delicacy and customer service, as well as entertainment and leisure areas such as children's paradise.

According to statistics, Haitang bay duty-free shopping center has introduced nearly 300 internationally renowned brands and over 100, 000 fashion items. Among them, more than ten brands such as Prada, Giorgio Armani and Rolex have entered the duty-free market in mainland China for the first time, and the global flagship stores and concept stores of perfume, cosmetics, tourism and retail markets such as Chanel, Dior, Estee Lauder, Lancôme and other top brands will also meet consumers for the first time. Rich categories and brands not only can provide consumers with more choices, fully meet the flagship needs of tourism, but also bring the offshore duty-free shopping to a new level.

In addition to enjoying the pleasure of travel shopping, consumers can also experience a unique "flower watching trip" in the shopping center. The architectural design of shopping center is inspired by the Chinese flowering crabapple. The overall building adopts the continuous space curved steel structure, just like a beautiful "Chinese flowering crabapple" blooming in the blue coastline. Combined with the five senses of commercial shopping, namely vision, sound, smell, touch and appreciation, the overall project is designed as different theme pavilions of "sea, begonia, flower and treasure in the sea", and the interior space design also skillfully combines art community and fashion elements. No matter it is beautiful "crabapple" amorous feelings, or the unique interior design, will bring distinctive sensory impact and cheerful shopping enjoyment for the visitor.

In the past three years since the implementation of the duty-free policy on southern islands, the consumption of tourists in Hainan has changed significantly, and the proportion of shopping expenditure has rapidly increased from 13.8% to 27.6%. The duty-free policy on south islands has become a new name card of Hainan tourism. In the past, Hainan tourism, which mainly focused on tourism, is now changing to develop both tourism and shopping. The completion of Haitang bay duty-free shopping center will bring the offshore islands duty-free shopping into a new realm with its super scale, super brands and advanced services. The six tourism elements of "eat, live, transportation, travel, purchase and entertainment" will be improved. The opening of Haitang bay duty-free shopping center marks the development of China's duty-free industry to a new height. It provides a new platform for Chinese consumers to experience world-class duty-free shopping without going abroad.

After reading, please answer the questions below:

1. What does Haitang bay duty-free shopping center provide for our customers in the five functional zones?

2. How many renowned brands and items have been introduced? Take some for example.

3. What is the specialty of architectural design in Haitang bay shopping center?

4. What is the exact change from the implementation of duty-free policy on South Island?

5. What's the influence of the opening of Haitang bay duty-free shopping center?

Part III Listening

Listen to *dialogues* and finish the tasks.

Situational dialogue 1

Context: Shirley is a salesgirl in a duty-free shop at the airport; she is ready to provide service to Eric.

Task: answer the questions below.
1. Who does Eric buy gifts for?
2. Where is Eric from?
3. How much do the perfume in 30ml and 50ml cost respectively?
4. What does Eric finally prefer?

Shirley: Can I help you, sir? Would you like to buy some duty-free sales?
Eric: Yes, please. I am looking for some gifts for my wife.
Shirley: What kind of present do you want?
Eric: I am not sure. Do you have anything you can recommend?
Shirley: What about perfume, skincare product or something else?
Eric: I think my wife would like a bottle of perfume.
Shirley: That's good. I recommend you a good one. It's the brand of DKNY. That is very expensive in America.
Eric: Hey, how did you know I came from America?
Shirley: Just a hunch, sir. We have it in 30ml and 50ml.which do you prefer?
Eric: How much?
Shirley: Small one is 45 dollars, and the bigger one is just 60 dollars.
Eric: OK, I will take the bigger one, please.

Situational dialogue 2

Context: Shirley is a salesgirl in a duty-free shop at the airport; she is ready to provide service to Joyce.

Tasks: answer the questions below.
1. What product does Shirley recommend to Joyce?
2. What does Joyce want to buy?
3. How much does the product Joyce want to choose?
4. What kind of payment doses Joyce prefer?

Shirley: Excuse me madam, would you like to buy some duty-free goods? We have many quality products from the word's well-known brands.

Joyce: What do you have?

Shirley: Different kinds of cosmetics, jewelries and watches and so on. Here is the duty-free guide.

Joyce: I'd like to have this lipstick. Was it made in France?

Shirley: Yes, Madam. It was originally made in France.

Joyce: Good. How much is it?

Shirley: It costs 180 yuan.

Joyce: OK.

Shirley: Are you paying by credit card or cash?

Joyce: Credit card.

Shirley: Thank you, Madam. Here is your receipt.

Joyce: OK. Thanks.

Shirley: You are welcome.

Situational dialogue 3

Context: Shirley is a salesgirl in a duty-free shop at the airport; she is assisting a customer David with his selection.

Task: answer the questions below.
1. What duty-free item does David want to purchase?
2. What's the reason why David decide not to buy 300 sticks of Zhonghua?
3. How much the products cost altogether?
4. Why David's credit card is not allowed to use?

Shirley: Would you like to have some duty-free items, sir.

David: Hmm. Let me see. I'll have 300 Zhonghua and 2 bottles of Maotai, please.

Shirley: I'm sorry, sir. Visitors are only allowed to bring into China 2 sets of cigarettes which is 200 sticks or 50 cigars at most for one's duty-free. Otherwise you have to pay the customs taxes.

David: OK, I'll have 200.

Shirley: OK, sir. Let me see. 200 sticks of Zhonghua is 1000 yuan, and 2 bottles of Maotai is 1800 yuan, it comes to 2800 yuan. How would you like to pay?

David: By credit card. Do you take American Express?

Shirley: Of course, sir. Just a moment, please. I'm sorry, sir. But your card has expired. we can't accept it. Do you have another one, or would you like to pay by cash?

David: I'm terribly sorry. Let's do cash. Here you are.

Shirley: Thank you very much, sir.

Part IV Vocabulary

Textbook	Word stress	Translation
catalogue	CA-ta-lo-gue	目录
cosmetic	cos-ME-tic	化妆品
fragrance	FRAG-ran-ce	香水
accessory	ac-CE-sso-ry	小饰品；配件
confectionery	con-FEC-tion-ery	糖果点心
liquor	Li-quor	烈酒
tobacco	to-Ba-cco	烟草
boutique	bou-TI-que	精品；精品店
change	CHan-ge	找零
cash	CAsh	现金
debit card	DE-bit card	借记卡
credit card	CRE-dit card	信用卡
unionpay	U-nion PAY	银联卡
perfume	PER-fume	香水
cologne	co-LO-gne	古龙水
skincare product	SKIN-care PRO-duct	护肤品
expire	ex-PIRE	期满；到期；终止
discount	dis-COUNT	折扣
duty-free items	Du-ty free I-tems	免税商品
currency	CUR-ren-cy	货币
sought-after	sought-AF-ter	受欢迎的
purchase	PUR-cha-se	购买；采购
receipt	re-CEIpt	收据
jewelry	JEW-el-ry	珠宝
commodity	co-MMO-di-ty	商品；物品
delicacy	DE-li-ca-cy	美味佳肴
paradise	PA-ra-di-se	天堂
architectural	AR-chi-TEC-tural	建筑的
inspire	in-SPI-re	激发；鼓励；产生灵感
crabapple	crab-A-pple	海棠
pavilion	pa-VI-lion	馆；阁，亭子
begonia	be-GO-nia	棠（海棠花）
amorous	A-mo-rous	多情的，热情的
sensory	SEN-so-ry	感觉的；知觉的

阅读译文

全球最大的免税店——海棠湾免税购物中心

三亚海棠湾免税购物中心总建筑面积约12万平方米，商业面积达7.2万平方米，是全球规模最大的单体免税店。超大的购物中心包含了多种业态，也拥有更多的功能体验。路易威登（Louis Vuitton）、普拉达（Prada）、乔治阿玛尼（Giorgio Armani）等众多国际顶级品牌入驻，还汇集了各国特色商品、海南特产、户外运动、美食、顾客服务五大功能分区，兼有儿童乐园等娱乐休闲区域。

据统计，海棠湾免税购物中心共计引进了近300个国际知名品牌，超100,000个时尚单品。其中，普拉达（Prada）、乔治阿玛尼（Giorgio Armani）、劳力士（Rolex）等十多个品牌是首次进入中国大陆免税市场渠道，Chanel、Dior、Estee Lauder、Lancome等顶级品牌的香水化妆品旅游零售市场全球旗舰店与概念店也首次与消费者见面。丰富的品类、品牌能为消费者提供更多方面的选择，充分满足旅游购物的需求，也将离岛免税购物带上一个新的台阶。

除了享受旅游购物的乐趣外，消费者还能在购物中心体验一次独特的"赏花之旅"。购物中心建筑设计灵感源于有着"国艳"之称的海棠花，整体建筑采用连续空间曲面钢结构，如同一朵娇艳的"海棠花"盛开在蔚蓝海岸线上。结合商业购物的五感，即视觉、听觉、嗅觉、触觉、味觉，整体项目设计为"海、棠、花、海中瑰宝"不同的主题馆，而室内空间设计也将艺术群落与时尚元素巧妙结合。不论是美轮美奂的"海棠"风情，还是独具匠心的室内设计，都将为游客带来独特的感官冲击和愉悦的购物享受。

Part V Discussion

1. What did you learn from this unit?

2. Suppose you are a salesman in a duty-free shop, a foreign customer wants to buy a Chinese specialty as a gift for his friend. How to offer recommendation and service? You can prepare a dialogue according to the situation.

3. Discuss with your partners about the procedure and qualification of claiming to a tax refund for overseas visitors.

Part VI Writing

According to what you have learned in this unit, try to fill the Refund Application form for Overseas Visitors.

Module 5 Airport Service   135

境外旅客购物离境退税申请单
Refund Application Form for Overseas Visitors

商店名称（章）：　　　　　　开单日期：　年　月　日
Name of Retailer(Stamp)　　　　Date　　Y.　M.　D.　No.

姓名 Full Name of Applicant		证件类型 Passport Type		证件号码 Passport Number		
证件签发国 / 地区 Passport Issued by(Country/Region)			入境时间 Date of Entry into China			

商品明细 Items for Refund									
序号 Number	商品名称 Name of Goods	数量 Quantity	计量单位 Unit	单价 Unit Price	金额 Amount Paid	退税率 Refund Rate	退税额 Amount To be Refunded	旅客申报退税数量 Declared Quantity	备注 Remarks
1									
2									
3									
4									
5									
6									
7									
8									
9									
10									
11									
12									
合计 Total									

旅客退税申请 Tourist Application	1. 退税方式：　　现金□　　　转账□　　开户行：　　　　　　　银行账号： Refund Mode:　　Cash　　Bank Transfer　Bank Name＿＿＿＿＿＿　Account No. ＿＿＿＿＿ 2. 退税币种：　　人民币　　美元　　欧元　　日元 Preferred Currency　RMB □　　USD □　　EUR □　　JPY □ 3. 电话：　　　　　　　　　　　旅客签名： 4. Tel＿＿＿＿＿＿＿＿＿＿＿＿＿　Applicant's Signature　　　　日期：　年　月　日 　　　　　　　　　　　　　　　　　　　　　　　　　　　　　　　　Date　　Y.　M.　D.
海关验收情况 Customs Approval	经办人：　　　　　　　　　　签章： Official　　　　　　　　　　Stamp 旅客签名：　　　　　　　　　　　　　　　　　　　　　日期：　年　月　日 Applicant's Signature　　　　　　　　　　　　　　　　Date　　Y.　M.　D.

Unit 17 In-flight Service

Learning objectives

1. Know how to welcome on board and settle passengers;
2. Know how to provide beverage and meal services;
3. Know how to provide entertainment service;
4. Know how to deal with problems and complaints about other passengers;
5. Master the useful words and expressions about in-flight services.

Part I Warming up

1. Look at the boarding pass below. What information is printed here?

2. Label the objects in the cabin. Use these words.
arm-rest LCD screen head-rest overhead locker/bin tray table seat-belt
overhead light instruction light trolley reclining seat

_____   _____   _____

  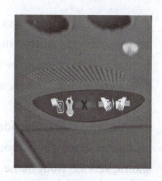

"Emirates' First Class product is an end-to-end experience."
(阿联酋航空的一流产品是终端到终端的体验。)

President of Emirates Airline
——Tim Clark

Part II Reading

Emirates airlines wins world's best first class airline

Emirates is the largest airline in the Middle East, operating more than 2,400 passenger flights a week from its hub at Dubai International Airport terminal 3 to 105 cities in 62 countries on six continents. Emirates Airlines has been named the world's best First Class airline at the Trip Advisor Traveler Choice® Awards 2019. The airline also won several other awards, including Best Middle East Business Class, Best Middle East First Class, and the honor of best Middle East Passenger Choice airline. Trip Advisor ranks the world's top airlines based on the number and quality of airline reviews and ratings by Trip Advisor flyers, collected over the past 12 months.

Emirates' first-class experience has defined innovations in premium travel products, such as private suites, in-flight showers and spas, in-flight lounges. The airline's newest first-class cabin features a fully enclosed private suite inspired by Mercedes-Benz, sliding doors and stylish design, soft and comfortable leather seats, high-tech controls and emotional lighting.

Sir Tim Clark, President of Emirates, said: 'Emirates' first class product offers passengers a carefree experience throughout the flight.From the ground service before flight, including the shuttle service from home to the airport, the exclusive check-in counter, the exclusive Emirates lounge of the airport, to the comfortable experience brought by all the onboard products and services.From an early age, Emirates has been a leader in delivering a superior first class experience, while investing in products and innovation. "We are delighted to receive this award and to see how our superior first class experience has been loved and recognized by our passengers."

With Emirates, travelers can enjoy the award-winning comfortable experience and intimate service, including teams of flight attendants from different countries and regions, more than 4,000 channels available on demand, in flight entertainment systems that bring passengers interesting movies, songs and games, as well as meals and free drinks with local characteristics. Passengers travelling with children will also enjoy Emirates' exclusive products and special care for their families.

After reading, please answer these questions below:
1. What kind of awards does Emirates obtain in 2019?
2. What are the features in first class cabin of Emirates?
3. What are the social rank and influence of Emirates?
4. What is the core competence of Emirates?

Part III   Listening

Listen to *dialogues* and finish the tasks.

Situational dialogue 1

Context: Lily is a flight attendant, she is welcoming on board and settling passengers in the cabin.

Task: answer the questions below.
1. Where is David's seat?
2. Why does Lily advise David to put his baggage somewhere else?
3. What problem does David put forward?

Lily: Good morning, sir. Welcome on board.
David: Good morning.

Lily: Excuse me, sir. Could you please step aside and allow the other passengers to go through?

David: Sorry. But I am not sure where my seat is?

Lily: Business class or economy? May I see your boarding pass, sir?

David: Economy. Here you are.

Lily: Your seat number is 18C. Well, it is in the middle of the cabin, the aisle seat. This way please. I will show you your seat.

David: Thank you so much.

Lily: You are welcome, sir. Would you mind me putting your baggage somewhere else? Your bag is too heavy. It might fall down in case of turbulence and hurt somebody.

David: OK. But I have another problem, my wife and I got separate seats, but we want to sit together.

Lily: Would you please take the seat assigned to you for the time being? I'll try to let you sit together. I'll ask if that passenger mind moving to another seat.

David: OK. It is very kind of you.

Situational dialogue 2

Context: Tom is a flight attendant; he is providing beverage and meal services in the cabin.

Tasks: answer the questions below.

1. What kind of meals do Joyce and his husband want to order?
2. Why can't Tom meet Joyce's needs for the first time?
3. What kind of food does Joyce finally choose?
4. What kind of drinks doses the Joyce prefer finally?

Tom: Excuse me, Madam. What would you like to eat?

Joyce: I'd like noodles and my husband would like rice, please.

Tom: I am sorry Madam. This is a short-haul flight. I am afraid we only have snacks.

Joyce: Then, do you have some peanuts or sandwiches?

Tom: Yes, we have. What kinds of sandwiches would you like, Madam, cheese or ham?

Joyce: Cheese, please.

Tom: Would you like something to drink, madam?

Joyce: Yes. What is available on board?

Tom: We have tea, coffee, Cola, fruit juice and mineral water. Which would you prefer?

Joyce: two cups of coffee for my husband and me, please.

Tom: How do you like your coffee, with cream or sugar?

Joyce: No thanks. We'd like to have black coffee. And make it very strong, please.

Tom: OK. No sugar, no cream and very strong. Here you are. Enjoy!

Joyce: Thank you very much.

Tom: My pleasure.

Situational dialogue 3

Context: Lily is a flight attendant; she is dealing with problems with some passengers when inspecting the cabin.

Task: answer the questions below.

1. Where does David want to go?
2. Why does Lily persuade David return to his seat?
3. What's the matter with Tom?
4. What suggestion does Lily give to Joyce?

Lily: Excuse me, sir. Would you please return to your seat?

David: Why? I am going to the lavatory.

Lily: Sorry, sir. For your safety you must remain in your seat with your seat belt fastened during turbulence. Please refrain from using the lavatories until the seat belt sign is switched off.

David: All right. I will go back to my seat.

Lily: Thank you for your cooperation.

(Lily is inspecting in the cabin and finding there is something wrong with the man.)

Lily: May I help you, Sir?

Tom: Yes. I am feeling sick and dizzy.

Lily: Really. I think you are suffering from airsickness. You need to take some hot water. You can decline your seat back and have a rest. Please wait a bit. Here is a glass of water. If you want to vomit, please use the air-sick bag in the seat pocket in front of you.

Tom: Thank you. That's very thoughtful of you.

Lily: you are welcome. If there's anything I can do for you, just press the call button.

Tom: Many thanks!

Situational dialogue 4

Context: Lily is a flight attendant; she is dealing with some complaints from a passenger.

Task: answer the questions below.

1. Why is David angry and complaining?
2. What does David want to do?
3. What does Lily suggest David to do?
4. How does flight attendant Lily solve the problem?
5. How does Lily tell the guy to use the headphones?

David: Excuse me, the group of people is making too much noise, they are disturbing me and everyone around. If you can't do anything about it, you will have to find another seat. I refuse to sit here any longer.

Lily: Yes, I understand. I can hear how noisy they are, and I am sorry that they are disturbing you. Have you spoken to them yourself?

David: Of course not. I don't think they care about me or anyone else.

Lily: Let me have a word with them. If it doesn't get better, then I will try to find you another seat, although the plane is pretty full. How about that?

David: Well, yes. Thank you. That would be fine.

(Lily is taking with the noisy group.)

Lily: Excuse me, excuse me. Listen, guys, are you enjoying the flight?

Man 1: You bet. It is great.

Lily: Great. Could I ask you a special favor? Would you mind just keeping your voices down a little? You are getting a little loud and some people are trying to sleep and watch a film.

Man2: Are we making a lot of noise?

Lily: But actually we can hear you all in the galley.

Man2: OK, no problem.

Lily: Thank you for your cooperation. We have some classical music; would you like to try?

Man 1: Sure. But do you know how to use these headphones?

Lily: Let me show you how to use the headset. You can put the jack plug into the socket and turn the knob like this. And you can get different programs on the channels.

Man 1: Oh I see. Let me try.

Lily: Is that OK?

Man 1: Yes, very clear. Thank you.

Situational dialogue 5

Context: Tom is a flight attendant; he is looking around the cabin before landing.

Task: answer the questions below.

1. What does Tom suggest Joyce to do?
2. How to stow the tray table?
3. Before landing, what are all the passengers required to do?

Tom: Excuse me, madam. Would you please return your seat back to the upright position and stow your tray table? We will be landing soon.

Joyce: All right. But I don't know how to stow my tray table.

Tom: Let me help you. Just put it upright and turn this knob tightly. Now it is appropriately stowed.

Joyce: Thank you.

(At this moment, the chief attendant is making a landing announcement.)

Ladies and gentlemen,

We will be landing at Shuangliu International Airport shortly. Before you go through

Customs and immigration, you must fill in the arrival form and the Custom declaration form. In order to speed your passage through Customs, we will distribute the forms to you to complete before landing. If you have any question about the forms, please ask a cabin attendant for help. For your safety, please remain seated and ensure that your seat belt is fastened. At last, on behalf of the crew, I would like to thank you all for your cooperation and wish you a pleasant journey in Chengdu. Thank you!

Part IV Vocabulary

Textbook	Word stress	Translation
cabin	CA-bin	客舱
cabin attendant	CA-bin a-TTEN-dant	客舱乘务员
overhead locker	over-HEAD LO-ker	头顶行李箱
window blind	WIN-dow blind	客舱的遮光板
ascend	a-SCEND	爬升
descend	de-SCEND	下降
depart	de-PART	离开；出发
cruise	cru-ise	巡航
altitude	AL-ti-tu-de	高度
navigation system	na-vi-GA-tion SYS-tem	导航系统
taxi	TAX-i	滑行
turbulence	TUR-bu-len-ce	颠簸
decompression	DE-com-PRE-ssion	减压；失压
buckle	BU-ckle	系上（安全带）
unbuckle	un-BU-ckle	解开（安全带）
luggage	LUG-ga-ge	行李
suitcase	SUIT-case	手提箱
briefcase	BRIE-f-ca-se	公文包
carry-on baggage	CAR-ry on BAG-ga-ge	随身行李
hand baggage	hand BAG-ga-ge	手提行李
checked baggage	check-ed BAG-ga-ge	托运行李
valuables	VA-lu-a-bles	贵重物品
belongings	be-LONG-ing-s	随身财物
baggage claim tag	BAG-ga-ge claim tag	行李牌
stow	STOW	将某物装好收起
offload	off-LOAD	卸下
oversize	OV-er-si-ze	过大

Module 5　Airport Service　143

Textbook	Word stress	Translation
symptom	SYM-P-tom	症状
fragile	FRA-gi-le	易碎的
airsick	AIR-sick	晕机的
airsickness bag	AIR-SICK-ness bag	呕吐袋
vomit	VO-mit	呕吐
dizzy	DI-zzy	使人眩晕的
choke	cho-ke	窒息；哽咽；阻塞
bruise	bru-ise	碰伤；擦伤
boarding pass	BOAR-ding pass	登机牌
assigned seat	a-SSIGN-ed seat	指定座位
embark	em-BARK	上机；上船
disembark	dis-em-BARK	下机；下船
tray table	tray ta-ble	小桌板
staple food	STA-ple food	主食
main course	main cour-se	主菜
dessert	de-SSERT	甜点；甜品
refreshment	re-FRESH-ment	点心
pastry	PAS-try	茶点
beverage	BE-ve-ra-ge	饮料
vegetarian meal	ve-ge-TA-rian meal	素食餐
diabetic meal	dia-BE-tic meal	无糖餐
mineral water	MI-ner-al WA-ter	矿泉水
juice	ju-ice	果汁；果汁饮料
soda water	SO-da WA-ter	苏打水；气泡水
cutlery	CUT-lery	餐具（特指刀、叉、勺、匙）
tableware	TA-ble-ware	餐具（包括碗、盘、刀叉等）
trolley	TRO-lley	餐车；手推车
wet tissue	wet TI-ssue	湿纸巾
passport	PASS-port	护照；通行证
visa	VI-sa	（护照等的）签证；背签
signature	SIG-na-ture	署名；签字
terminal	TER-mi-nal	航站楼
lounge	loun-ge	休息室
chauffeur	CHAU-ffeur	司机
hospitality	hos-pi-TA-li-ty	好客，殷勤
aviation	A-vi-A-tion	航空，飞机制造业
profitability	PRO-fi-ta-BI-li-ty	收益性，盈利能力

阅读译文

阿联酋航空公司荣获全球最佳头等舱荣誉称号

阿联酋航空公司是中东地区最大的航空公司,每周运营2400多次客运航班,从位于迪拜国际机场3号航站楼的枢纽机场飞往6大洲62个国家的105个城市。阿联酋航空公司在2019年旅行顾问旅行者选择®大奖中荣获全球最佳头等舱。该航空公司还获得了其他几个奖项,包括最佳中东地区商务舱、最佳中东头等舱,并获得了中东地区最佳旅客选择航空公司的荣誉。trip advisor根据旅行者在过去12个月里收集的航空公司评论和评级的数量和质量,评选出了全球排名靠前的航空公司。

阿联酋航空的头等舱体验定义了高端旅游产品的创新,如私人套房、飞机上的淋浴Spa、飞机上的休息室。该航空公司最新的头等舱采用了全封闭式私人套房,灵感来自梅赛德斯-奔驰(Mercedes-Benz),搭配落地滑动门及富有时尚感的设计,配备柔软舒适的皮质座椅、高科技控制面板和情绪照明系统。

阿联酋航空总裁蒂姆·克拉克爵士表示:"阿联酋航空的头等舱产品为乘客提供贯穿整个飞行的无忧体验。从飞行前的地面服务,包括从家门口到机场的专车接送服务、专属值机柜台、机场的阿联酋航空专属候机室,到全部机上产品和服务所带来的舒适体验。很久以前,阿联酋航空便成为打造出色头等舱体验的领导者,同时在产品和创新上不断投入,我们十分高兴能够获得这一奖项,并看到我们卓越的头等舱体验受到了乘客的喜爱和认可。"

搭乘阿联酋航空,全舱乘客都可以享受到屡获殊荣的舒适体验和贴心服务,包括来自不同国家和地区的空乘团队,包括4000多个可点播频道,为乘客带来好看好玩的影片、歌曲和游戏的机上娱乐系统,以及极具地方特色的餐食和免费饮品。携带儿童出行的乘客还能享受到阿联酋航空为家庭乘客提供的专属产品和特别关怀。

Part V　Discussion

1. What did you learn from this unit?
2. If you have a chance to be a flight attendant, what qualities do you have?
3. How to provide high-quality service to passengers in the cabin?
4. Discuss with your partners about how to fill the arrival card and departure card for overseas visitors.

Part VI　Writing

According to what you have learned in this unit, try to fill the Arrival Card and Departure Card.

外国人入境卡

ARRIVAL CARD

请交边防检查官员查验

For Immigration clearance

姓 _____ 名 _____
Family name   Given names

国籍 _____ 护照号 _____
Nationality   Passport No.

在华住址 _____
Intended address in China

出生日期 |___|___|___| 年year |___|___| 月month |___|___| 日day
date of Birth

签证号码 _____
Visa No.

签证签发地 _____
Place of visa issuance

航班号/船名/车次 _____
Flight No./Ship's name/Train No.

男 □ 女 □
male   female

入境事由（只能填写一项） Purpose of visit(one only)
访问 □   观光/休闲 □
Visit   Sightseeing/In leisure
会议/商务 □   学习 □
Conference/Business Study
就业 □   其他 □
Employment   Others
探亲访友 □
Visiting friends
定居 □
Settle down
返回常住地 □
Return home

以上申明真实准确。   签名：Signature _____
I hereby declare that the statement given above is true and accurate.

外国人出境卡
DEPARTURE CARD

请交边防检查官员查验
For Immigration clearance

姓 Family name _____

名 Given names _____

护照号码 Passport No. _____

出生日期 Date of Birth 年 year ____ 月 month ____ 日 day ____

男 □ male　　女 □ female

国籍 Nationality _____

航班号/船名/车次 Flight No./Ship's name/Train No. _____

以上申明真实准确。
I hereby declare that the statement given above is true and accurate.

签名: Signature _____

妥善保留此卡, 如遗失将会对出境造成不便。
Retain this card in your possession, failure to do so may delay your departure from China.

Module 6
Customer Relationship Management

Unit 18 Calling for Feedback

 Learning objectives

1. Know how to make and answer inquiries in English.
2. Master the words and expressions concerning customer survey.
3. Know how to deal with customers' inquiries.

Part I Warming up

Task: Complete the following survey form about the hotel restaurant.

CUSTOMER SATISFACTION SURVEY

The Sunshine Hotel Restaurant is committed to customer satisfaction and would like to know how well we are doing. Your answer will help to improve our service. Thank you for your time and comments.

1. Restaurant hours are convenient.
    Strongly agree   Agree   Neutral   Disagree   Strongly Disagree
2. The choice of food is wide.
    Strongly agree   Agree   Neutral   Disagree   Strongly Disagree
3. Prices are reasonable.
    Strongly agree   Agree   Neutral   Disagree   Strongly Disagree
4. Food is tasty.
    Strongly agree   Agree   Neutral   Disagree   Strongly Disagree
5. How satisfied or dissatisfied are you with the quality of the food?
    Very Satisfied   Satisfied   Neither Satisfied Nor Dissatisfied
    Dissatisfied   Very Dissatisfied
6. How satisfied or dissatisfied are you with the environment of the items in our restaurant?
    Very Satisfied   Satisfied   Neither Satisfied Nor Dissatisfied
    Dissatisfied   Very Dissatisfied
7. How satisfied or dissatisfied are you with the restaurant?
    Very Satisfied   Satisfied   Neither Satisfied Nor Dissatisfied
    Dissatisfied   Very Dissatisfied

   All the information you provide will be anonymous and be treated confidentially. Thank you!

"We must accept finite disappointment, but we must never lose infinite hope."
（我们必须接受失望，因为它是有限的，但千万不可失去希望，因为它是无穷的。）

——Mattin Luther King

Part Ⅱ Reading

The Art of Slow Travel

In Namibia a year earlier, I realized that one of the sovereign blessings of the place is that, in nine days and nights, I had barely gone online and had made and received exactly one phone call (to my wife, to remind her when I would be coming home). And, of course, in the presence of desert-adapted rhinos and sand dunes the height of skyscrapers, I had never begun to miss the tiny screen.

More and more people are spending hundreds of pounds a night to stay in "black-hole resorts," one of whose main attractions is that you hand over your smartphone and tablet on arrival. In a world where the human race accumulates more information every five minutes than exists in the entire US Library of Congress, emptiness and silence are the new luxuries.

Welcome, in short, to "slow travel," which comes to seem ever more tempting in an age of acceleration. This can take the form of merely unplugging; but it also speaks for the special, everyday allure of seeing somewhere on foot, of going to one place (and not 10) in 14 days, and sometimes of going somewhere to do nothing at all. This used to be known as idling, but in a multi-tasking world, in which we seem to be living at a pace dictated by machines, going at human speed suddenly begins to look like sanity and freedom.

I experienced my first taste of slow travel 23 years ago, when I checked into a monastery, of all places—even though years of the enforced chapel at school had left me all but allergic to church services. It didn't matter. The chance to take walks, to forget about phone calls, to sit and just catch my breath, so invigorated me that when I moved to Japan, I took a two-room flat that had something of the quiet of a retreat house.

But I also experienced a sense of freedom when I arrived in Zurich, to find I could get everywhere by easy and frequent tram. I've known friends take tours on bicycles, or long train rides so they can simply read and write and chat with strangers. I've seen them go skiing in Kashmir, where there's just one chairlift, or fishing in Scotland or Montana to catch some stillness. Even Ritz-Carltons and InterContinental's now offer "digital detox" packages to help open your eyes and ears to the wonders around you.

The essence of holidays, and therefore travel, is to get what you don't get enough of the rest of the time. And for more and more of us, this isn't a movement, diversion or stimulation; we've got plenty of that in the palms of our hands. It's the opposite: the chance to make contact with loved ones, to be in one place and to enjoy the intimacy and sometimes life-changing depth of talking to one person for five—or 15—hours.

Of course, lying on a beach or in a hammock has always offered something of a respite from the rat race. But as I hear of westerners walking to Mount Kailash, or a film producer going to Seychelles just to read books with his daughter. As I see how the appeal of a long walk in the woods is not just the woods but the lack of all signals, I suspect that the world had reversed direction since the time, not so long ago, when jumbo jets and Concordes first promised to whisk us across the planet at supersonic speeds. Concorde, after all, is gone now; but near where I live, in the old Japanese capital of Nara, there are more and more rickshaws in view—to cater to the very people who patented the idea of "Six Cities in Four Days."

After reading, please answer these questions below:
1. Is it a bad news for the writer?
2. According to the passage, what's the "black-hole resorts"?
3. Do you like the "slow travelling" mentioned in this passage, why?

Part Ⅲ Listening

Listen to dialogues and finish the tasks.
Situational dialogue 1
Listen to the conversation between Eric and a travel agency worker and tick the correct answer to each question.

1. Who influence Eric most as to choosing the travel agency?
   A. His parents
   B. His friends
   C. Nobody

2. What is the advantage of Sunshine Travel Agency compared with Amazing Travel Agency?
   A. Sunshine Travel Agency is cheaper
   B. Sunshine Travel Agency offers more choices
   C. Sunshine Travel Agency stands out among the other travel agencies

3. What's the important factor in Eric's purchasing decision?
   A. The price
   B. The free gift with purchase
   C. The products itself

Worker: Excuse me. I'm from the Customer Service Department of Sunshine Travel Agency. I wonder if you'd mind answering a few questions about our traveling products.

Eric: OK. No problem.

Worker: Thanks. First, why did you choose our products?

Eric: Well, I don't have much time. One of my friends told me your products are quite good, so I chose it.

Worker: Are you satisfied with your journey? And which part are you satisfied most with?

Eric: I'm very satisfied with this journey in Beijing. I think your arrangement of the travel itinerary is thoughtful.

Worker: Have you ever used other company's product?

Eric: I had a journey arranged by Amazing Travel Agency.

Worker: If you compare these two travel agency, which one do you prefer?

Eric: Well, both are very good---Sunshine offers more choices.

Worker: Do you think price is an important factor in your purchasing decision?

Eric: Not so much. I only buy products that make me feel good.

Worker: Well, thank you very much. Your opinions are very valuable to us.

Situational dialogue 2

Rose Taylor is conducting an opinion survey on the Sunshine Hotel. Listen to the conversation and answer the following questions.

1. What are Rose doing now?
2. Which aspect of the hotel are the man satisfied most with?
3. Which aspect of the hotel are the man not satisfied with?
4. Does the man think the room rate is reasonable? Why?

Rose: Excuse me, Sir. My name is Rose Taylor. I am working in the Customer Service Department of Sunshine Hotel. Would you have time to answer a few questions?

Customer: What is it for?

Rose: We are conducting an opinion survey on whether customers are happy with our hotel's service.

Customer: Well, I would be glad to.

Rose: Which aspect of the hotel are you satisfied most with, environment, service or meal?

Customer: I think the service at your hotel is outstanding. Everyone treats us like a family member.

Rose: And which part are you not satisfied with?

Customer: If the breakfast could have much more choices, it would be better.

Rose: Do you think the room rate is expensive?

Customer: The room rate is indeed a little more expensive than the hotels at the same level. But take its location, its service and the articles in the room into consideration, I think the rate is still reasonable.

Rose: Thank you so much! Your opinion is beneficial to us.

Part IV Vocabulary

Textbook	Word stress	Translation
iconic	i-CO-nic	符号的；图标的；偶像的
accumulate	a-CCU-mu-la-te	累积；积聚

Textbook	Word stress	Translation
resort	re-SORT	度假胜地；常去之地
rhino	RHI-no	犀牛（等于 rhinoceros）；钱；现金
encounter	en-COUN-ter	遭遇，邂逅；遇到
sovereign	SOVE-reign	至高无上的；有主权的
Namibia	na-MI-bia	纳米比亚（非洲西南部国家）
acceleration	ac-ce-le-RA-tion	加速，促进
allure	a-LLURE	诱惑力；引诱力；吸引力
Sanity	SA-ni-ty	明智；精神健全；通情达理
DPRK	Democratic People's Republic of Korea	朝鲜民主主义人民共和国

阅读译文

慢旅行的艺术

一年前在纳米比亚我就意识到，身在那个地方一个最大的好处是，在九天九夜的时间里，我几乎没上过网，而且只接打过一个电话(是打给我妻子的，为了提醒她我回家的时间)。当然，那里有适应沙漠环境的犀牛和高度堪比摩天大楼的沙丘可赏，我一点也没有想念手机那块小小的屏幕。

越来越多的人一个晚上花几百英镑在"黑洞度假区"度假。这类度假区的一大主要吸引力在于，客人一到就必须交出智能手机和平板电脑。在这个人类每五分钟积累的信息量要比整个美国国会图书馆馆藏还多的世界里，空闲和清静成了新的奢侈品。

简言之，欢迎加入"慢旅行"。在这个加速运转的时代，慢旅行似乎正变得越发具有吸引力。慢旅行的形式可以是简单的断网关机，但也可以是日常生活里一些别致的吸引人的活动，比如走路去看风景，花两周游一个(而非十个)地方，有时还包括到一个地方无所事事地待着。这一度被视为是游手好闲之举，但在这个一心多用的世界中，我们生活的步伐似乎全被机器操控，保持常人的节奏忽然开始显得明智而自由。

假日的本质，进言之，旅行的本质是获取你平时无福尽情消受的东西。对于越来越多的人来说，要享受的不是奔波、消遣或刺激——这些我们已从掌上设备中获得了很多，而是与之相反的东西：与挚爱的人接触的机会，待在一个地方的机会，跟一个人聊上5个或15个小时，享受那种亲密深谈的机会——这种深谈有时可以改变人的一生。

Part V Discussion

Work in pairs. Role-play a conversation between Tommy White who is conducting an opinion survey on travel choice and a passenger in the street. The survey should involve the following aspects.

> - Greeting
> - Short Self-introduction
> - Survey Issues
> - Thanks

Part VI Writing

Questionnaire

A questionnaire is a form containing a set of questions submitted to people to gain specific information. It is often used to ask people for their opinions, views, or suggestions on a theme. A questionnaire usually contains the following three parts:

1. Introduction: how to fulfil the questionnaire.

2. Questions: a series of questions related to the themes.

3. Appreciation: Thanks to people who have taken time and effort in filling the questionnaire.

There are some tips on how to organize the questions:

1. Don't be too long.

2. Don't use difficult jargon.

3. Be particular and specific.

4. Avoid asking negative questions, for example, "Don' you think the service is satisfying?"

5. Avoid asking double questions.

Sample

Questionnaire on People's Preference for Hotel Choice

We're studying people's preference for hotel choice. Please tick the answer(s) that is (are) most appropriate to you for each of the questions in this questionnaire truthfully.

1. What is your gender?

    A. Male   B. Female

2. How old are you?

    A. Under 20   B. 30~40   C. 40~50   D. 50 and over

3. What is your education background?

    A. Less than high-school Education   B. High-school Education

    C. College Education   D. Higher than College Education

4. What is your relationship status?

    A. Married   B. Single

5. Does your occupation allow you to travel a lot?

    A. Often   B. Occasionally   C. Never

6. What is the most important thing to consider when you choose a hotel?
   A. Cost   B. Brand   C. Location   D. Service
   E. Sanitary Condition   F. Meals   G. Safety Factor
   H. Environment   I. Others

7. If you're away from home, which types of hotel will you tend to choose?
   A. Star Hotels   B. Economy Hotels   C. Family Inn   D. Others

8. Which channel do you prefer to use to know the hotel information?
   A. Advertisements   B. Relatives and Friends   C. Books and Magazines about Travel
   D. Travel Apps   E. Others

All this information you provide will be anonymous and be treated confidentially. Thank you!

Task: Suppose you are hired by the marketing department of a travel agency and asked to prepare a questionnaire to determine college students' preference for travel. Please design a questionnaire and collect related information from your classmates.

Unit 19 | Dealing with Complaints

Learning objectives

1. Know how to handle complaints efficiently.
2. Master the useful expressions about Complaint letter.

Part I Warming up

Match the following customers' complaints with the clerks' responses.

Complaints
1. There is other people's hair on the bed.
2. I'm afraid there is something wrong in our bill. You overcharged me 10 yuan.
3. What's wrong? Our flight is half an hour late.
4. The pizza tastes too salty!

Responses
A. I'm sorry to hear that. I will ask our chef to cook you a new one.
B. I'm sorry for the delay, but your plane is held up by the air traffic control.
C. I will send someone to your room and have the sheet changed.
D. Let me check. There could have been some mistake. I'm sorry for it. Here is 10 yuan.

"Never put off till tomorrow what may be done today."
（今日事，今日毕。）
——Unknown

Part II Reading

Your Privacy at 30, 000ft

A passenger on a Singapore flight tweeted a photograph last week of the seat-back display, prompting other air travelers to voice concerns about their privacy at 30,000ft.

Three of the world's biggest airlines have admitted some of their planes have cameras installed on the backs of passenger seats. American Airlines, United Airlines and Singapore Airlines have new seat-back entertainment systems that include cameras. They could also be on planes used by other carriers.

Companies that make the entertainment systems are fitting them with cameras to offer passengers options such as seat-to-seat video conferencing, according to an American Airlines spokesman. But American, United and Singapore all say they have never activated the cameras and have no plans to use them.

While video conferencing is not available on United flights, the feature is currently in use on some Emirates flights with Panasonic entertainment systems aboard, for first-class fliers.

In a statement provided after publication, Panasonic Avionics Corporation said that it "will never activate any feature or functionality within an IFE system without explicit direction from an airline customer" and that "the cameras have simply been included to support potential future applications like seat-to-seat video conferencing."

Vitaly Kamluk, who photographed the camera on his flight, suggested that carriers should cover the lenses with stickers and said it would be easy for airlines to monitor passengers with them. "The cameras are probably not used now," he tweeted. "But if they are wired, operational, bundled with mic, it's a matter of one smart hack to use them on 84+ aircrafts and spy on passengers."

American Airlines spokesman Ross Feinstein said cameras were in "premium economy" seats on 82 Boeing 777 and Airbus A330-200 jets. Cameras are a standard feature on many in-flight entertainment systems used by multiple airlines, he said. British Airways told The Independent none of its planes had cameras on seat backs. Singapore spokesman James Boyd said cameras were on 84 Airbus A350s, Airbus A380s and Boeing 777s and 787s. However, a United spokeswoman repeatedly told reporters on Friday that none of its entertainment systems had cameras — before apologizing and saying that some did. The airlines stressed that they did not add the cameras — saying manufacturers embedded them in the entertainment systems.

After reading, please answer these questions below:

1. According to the airlines, what's the purpose of the cameras installed on the backs of passenger seats?
2. Why are the air travelers worried about their privacy at 30,000ft?

Part III Listening

Listen to *dialogues* and finish the tasks.
Situational dialogue 1
Eric Taylor is complaining to the hotel receptionist. Listen to the conversion and answer the

following questions.

1. What did Eric complaint about?
2. Were the rooms cleaning every day?
3. What is the receptionist's solution to the problem?
4. Were Eric satisfied with the solution? Why?

Eric: Excuse me.

Receptionist: How can I help you, sir?

Eric: We're regular guests at your hotel, but I'm about to change my mind about ever staying here again! The service is terrible. I've had to ring housekeeping every day to ask them to clean my room. My company pays good rates for my colleagues and me to stay at your hotel, so a dependable cleaning service is the least we expect!

Receptionist: First of all, I'd like to apologize on behalf of our hotel. So, if I understand you correctly, you had to call each day to get your room cleaned?

Eric: That's right.

Receptionist: Would you mind giving me some details? If I could just have your name, room number, what time you called and whom you spoke to exactly.

Eric: My name is Eric Taylor from room 1024, I have been calling every morning. I do not remember whom I spoke to.

Receptionist: Mr. Taylor, I'll speak to housekeeping straight away. Apologies for the inconvenience, I would like to offer you a free voucher for two nights stay on your next visit. You can use it any time you like.

Eric: Oh, that's great! I am glad that we could work this out. We will come back here again.

Situational dialogue 2

Eric Taylor is complaining to the hotel receptionist. Listen to the conversion and answer the following questions.

1. What is Eric complaint about?
2. What is the receptionist's solution to the problem?
3. Were Eric satisfied with the solution? Why?

Eric: Good morning!

Receptionist: Good morning, sir, how can I help you?

Eric: The people in the next room have loud parties every night and I have not been able to sleep. Also, the hotel bed is too hard.

Receptionist: I am so sorry sir; we had a group of guests here last night for a music festival.

Eric: It is not my fault.

Receptionist: Of course, sir. I will move you to another room and give you a free upgrade. May I have your name and room number?

Eric: Eric Taylor. I stay in room 1213.

Receptionist: Thank you Mr. Taylor, your new room is room 1412 on the 14th floor, it is a king size bed with softer mattress. You can move anytime tonight by getting the new room card from us. In addition, I would like to offer you a free buffet dinner in our hotel restaurant.

Eric: Well, thank you very much! I will get the key later.

Part IV Vocabulary & Notes

Textbook	Word stress	Translation
Tweet	tweet	推特；发推特
prompt	prompt	鼓励；促进；激起
entertainment	en-ter-TAIN-ment	娱乐；消遣；款待
embed	em-BED	栽种；使嵌入，使深留脑中
activate	AC-ti-vate	刺激；使活动；使活泼
functionality	func-tio-NA-li-ty	功能
available	a-VAIL-la-ble	可获得的；可找到的；有空的
application	a-ppli-CA-tion	应用；应用程序
IFE system	In-flight entertainment system	飞机客舱娱乐系统

Notes

The following are some sentences you can use when you are making or dealing with the complaints.

Useful expressions for a letter of complaint.

I am writing to complain about…
I am writing to express my dissatisfaction with…
We were disappointed with…
…was not what we had expected.
It didn't work/ was out of use.
I am not going to accept this/ put up with this.
It's high time you …
Unless…, we shall …
I should warn you that…

Complaining

I'd like to complain about…
I'm phoning to complain about…
There is something wrong with…
We've got a problem with…

I'm not happy with…
You said… but …

Apologizing

1. I do apologize./ I'm terribly sorry./ I'm extremely sorry. 实在抱歉。
2. Please accept our apology. 请接受我们的歉意。
3. Would you mind waiting a second? 您介意等一会儿吗？
4. I assure you it won't happen again. 我向您保证此类事件不会再发生。
5. I'm terribly sorry, I will fix the problem right away. 非常抱歉，我会马上处理这件事的。
6. Would you mind waiting a second? I will check it immediately. 您介意等一会儿吗？我马上就帮您查。
7. Thank you for your comments (compliment, suggestions). 感谢您的意见（赞扬、建议）。
8. Please accept my apologies on behalf of … 我代表…向您致歉。
9. I do apologize for the inconvenience on behalf of … 对给您造成的不便，我谨代表…向您道歉。

阅读译文

三万英尺高空的个人隐私

上周，新加坡航空公司的一位乘客在推特上传了一张座椅靠背显示屏的照片，促使其他乘客也表达了对3万英尺高空飞行中个人隐私的关注。全球最大的三家航空公司都已承认多个机型的座椅靠背上装有摄像头。

美国航空公司、联合航空公司和新加坡航空公司最新安装的座椅靠背娱乐系统中装有摄像头。其他航空公司的飞机上也可能安装了类似系统。

美国航空公司的一位发言人说，生产娱乐系统的公司安装摄像头是为了方便飞机乘客之间进行视频会议。不过，上述三家航空公司均表示他们从未启用那些摄像头，也没有计划使用。

联合航空公司的航班上还无法实现视频会议，但阿联酋航空公司一些航班的头等舱已经在使用这一技术，这些飞机上安装的是日本松下公司的系统。

松下航空电子公司发布声明说，"绝不会在未接到乘客明确指示的情况下，激活飞机客舱娱乐系统的任何功能。安装摄像头只是为了支持乘客间视频会议等未来的应用需求。"拍摄摄像头照片的乘客维塔利-卡姆卢克建议说，航空公司应该用贴纸盖住摄像头，有了摄像头，航空公司很容易监控乘客的一举一动。他在推特上说："摄像头可能现在还没有使用，但如果连上网，运行起来，再插上麦克风，就能成为超过84架飞机上的智能黑客系统，用来监视乘客。"

美国航空公司发言人罗斯-范斯坦说，82架波音777飞机和空客A330-200飞机"高级经济舱"的座椅靠背安装有摄像头。他说："摄像头是很多机内娱乐系统的标配，多家航空公司都在使用。"英国航空公司对《独立报》表示，并未在座椅靠背安装摄像头。新加坡航空公司发言人詹姆斯-博伊德说，84架空客A350、空客A380、波音777和787飞机上安装有摄像头。但联合航空公司的一位女发言人上周五反复对记者强调，飞机的娱乐系统中没有安装摄像头，但在此之后又承认了此事并表示道歉。航空公司强调说，摄像头并非公司安装，而是生产商将其内置进了娱乐系统。

Part V Discussion

Work in pairs. Practice making and handling a complaint with the given information below.
Role A There is no hot water in your room.
Role B The receptionist of the hotel.

Part VI Writing

Letter of Complaint

A letter of compliant requires payment for defective or damaged goods or poor services. It usually contains the following parts.

Background: describing the situation;
Problem: explaining the cause and effect;
Solution: stating what you want to be done about the problem;
Closing: ending with a wish to solve the problem.

The letter of complaint should be stated with necessary facts and be short, clear and polite.

Task: You had a horrible experience in a restaurant. Now you should write a complaint letter to the manager of the restaurant.

Sample

Dear Sir or Madam,

I'm writing to complain about the laundry service in your hotel.

I stayed in your hotel from December 25-28, 2018. And on the 25th, I had the laundry service. I had the sweater washed by the laundry department. However, when I got it back, the garment was stretched out of shape and no longer fits.I phoned the receptionist and tell him the incident, who was rather rude on the phone and informed me that I could not get any refund or a replacement sweater. I felt really upset, for I have been a loyal customer of your hotel for many years and until this incident, never have had any complaints. I, therefore, feel disappointed to be treated in such a manner.I would, however, be perfectly satisfied if you would kindly replace the sweater or refund my money, whichever is more convenient. Otherwise, I shall take matters further. I look forward to hearing from you soon.

Yours truly,
Eric Taylor

Unit 20 | Information Service

 Learning objectives

1. Know how to take good care of your valued clients.
2. Master the useful expressions about Adjustment letter.

Part I Warming up

Task: Decide which department should be responsible for the following complaints.
A. Shipping Department
B. Sales and Marketing Department
C. Accounting Department
D. Human Resources Department
E. Production Department
(　) 1. A mistake in an employee's salary
(　) 2. A defective product
(　) 3. Misleading advertisement
(　) 4. Rude attitude of a waiter
(　) 5. The delay of the product delivery

"A life without a purpose is a ship without a rudder."
（人生无目的，犹如船失舵。）

——Unknown

Part II Reading

The Restriction on the Number of the Travelers in Some Famous Scenic Spots

Travel these days involves exploring new destinations, eating new foods, making memories, and dodging tourists as they try to snap that perfect Instagram photo.

Instagram is great, but when Instagrammability becomes the No. 1 motivation for booking a holiday, and hotels start offering Instagram butlers, it can lead to over-tourism (a runner-up for word of the year!), dangerously crowded conditions, people making terrible choices to get a good shot, and a glut of articles about how Instagram is ruining travel. As the Instagram Effect continues into 2019, destinations are coming up with ways to fight back–and fight off the teeming hordes of selfie-stick-wielding visitors.

Here are five destinations fighting the Instagram Effect:

ISLE OF SKYE, SCOTLAND

Traveling Instagram influencers love snapping photos of the Isle of Skye's fairy pools, the sunset over Elgol, and the rocky Old Man of Storr.

The tiny island's infrastructure can't handle the traffic, leading to crowds, traffic jams, and misbehaving tourists. In 2017, local police on the Inner Hebridean island were warning people not to come if they didn't have accommodation booked.

DUBROVNIK, CROATIA

Thanks to Game of Thrones, the city's Old Town has been swamped with tourists snapping selfies in King's Landing. To combat the crowds, the city has limited the number of cruise ships that can dock and the number of visitors that can visit. In 2017, Dubrovnik limited the number of daily visitors to 8,000, monitored by security cameras, and new regulations expected to roll out in 2019 could halve that amount.

SKELLIG MICHAEL, IRELAND

Luke Skywalker's retreat in Star Wars: The Force Awakens has become an increasingly popular tourist destination–almost 17,000 visitors came in 2017. Now, the UNESCO World Heritage Site allows no more than 180 tourists per day and has been known to close to tourists to let nature have its way.

MALLORCA, SPAIN

Over-tourism on the Balearic island led to a "summer of action" where campaigners vandalized hotels, demonstrated at the airport, and tagged graffiti proclaiming that "tourism kills the city." The government responded by doubling the tourist tax to €4 ($4.64) per person per day, the Telegraph reports. It also cracked down on Airbnb and other short-term vacation rentals, "banning everything except those in detached homes that are neither on public land nor in a region near an airport," per CN Traveler.

MACHU PICCHU, PERUVIAN

In 2015, the Peruvian government announced its five-year, $43.7 million plan to protect the ruins, CN Traveler reports. In 2017, they started limiting tourists to two timed entries each day, requiring they be aided by an approved guide, and restricting them to specific trails through the ruins. Only 5,000 tickets are available each day, more than twice the number suggested by UNESCO. This year, they have further limited tourism, with a four-hour time limit and no re-entry allowed.

After reading, please answer these questions below:

1. What's the author's attitude towards Instagram?
2. What's the methods hold by the Isle of Skye to fight back and fight off the teeming hordes of selfie-stick-wielding visitors?

Part III   Listening

Listen to *dialogues* and finish the tasks.
Situational dialogue 1
Landy called Eric Taylor to invite him to a dinner. Listen to the conversation carefully and answer the following questions.
1. Why did Landy invite Mr Taylor to a dinner?
2. Did Mr Taylor agree to take part in the dinner?
3. What's the time and place for the dinner?

Landy: Good morning. This is Landy Ton from the Sunshine Hotel Customer Service Department. May I speak to Mr Taylor?
Eric: This is Mr Taylor speaking.
Landy: Mr Taylor you gave us some valuable feedback towards our service last month.
Eric: Oh, yes.
Landy: For showing our appreciation for your support to our hotel, we'd like to invite you to a dinner at our Hotel. When will you be available?
Eric: Thank you very much for inviting. I would love to come on Sunday.
Landy: That's great! We will be expecting you on this Sunday at our Hotel. And you may bring a guest with you. And I will be waiting for you at the lobby.
Eric: Thank you and see you then.

Situational dialogue 2
Rose called Eric Taylor to invite him to a tea party. Listen to the conversation carefully and answer the following questions.
1. Why did Rose invite Mr Taylor to a tea party?
2. What will they do in the tea party?
3. Did Mr Taylor agree to take part in the tea party?
4. What's the time and place for the tea party?

Rose: Hello! It is Rose Tan from Sunshine Travel Agency. May I speak to Mr Taylor?
Eric: Yes, I am speaking.
Rose: Hi, Mr Taylor. you have won a prize for filling out a questionnaire from our hotel. Do

you remember?

Eric: Yes.

Rose: Could I invite you to a tea party at the Sunshine Hotel on Saturday afternoon?

Eric: What is it for?

Rose: It is our company's annual event to thank representatives of our regular consumers.

Eric: Can I ask what we will do at the party?

Rose: First, you'll watch a fantastic dance performance while enjoying tea. Then we will have a show of our latest travel products. Each guest will have a gift.

Eric: Sounds very nice! I think I can manage to come on Saturday.

Rose: That would be great! We will be expecting you at 3:30p.m.. See you then!

Eric: Thanks. Goodbye!

Rose: Goodbye!

Part IV Vocabulary & Notes

Textbook	Word stress	Translation
Instagram	INS-ta-gram	照片分享（一款应用程序）
glut	glut	使…充满；使…吃饱；过多供应
teeming	TEE-ming	拥挤的，热闹的；多产的，丰富的
hoard	hoard	贮存（品），秘藏（品）
selfie-stick	selfie-stick	自拍杆
infrastructure	IN-fras-truc-ture	基础设施；公共建设
Accommodation	a-cco-mmo-DA-tion	住处，膳宿；预订铺位
swamp	swamp	使不堪承受，使疲于应对；淹没
combat	COM-bat	战斗；防止，抑制（尤用于新闻报道）
vandalize	VAN-da-lize	肆意毁坏；摧残（等于 vandalise）
graffiti	gra-FFI-ti	墙上乱写乱画的东西
crack	crack	破裂；打开

Notes

Letter of Adjustment

Letters of adjustment is the replies to letters of complaint, which must be handled carefully.

The following are some tips on writing letters of adjustment.

1. Mention the letters of complaints;

2. State the problem encountered by the customer;

3. If it's your company's fault, apologize;

4. Explain how the error occurred;

5. State exactly what you will do to solve the problem.

Useful expressions for a letter of adjustment

1. Thank you for your letter of …
2. I refer to your letter of…
3. We do apologize for…
4. Please accept our apologies for…
5. As a result of our investigation, we found that…
6. The error was caused by …
7. To show goodwill, we are preparing to …

阅读译文

著名景点限制游客量

如今的旅游，除了包括探索新的目的地、试吃新的食物、创造新的回忆，还包括一边躲避其他的游客一边试图拍出一张完美的 Ins 照。

Instagram 是挺好的，但是现在"可以发 Ins"已经成了度假的第一动力，而且酒店竟然还提供 Ins 管家，这就可能会导致旅游过剩的问题了(这都成了年度第二热词了)，还可能导致人群过挤而发生危险，人们为了拍一张好照片而做傻事，以及一堆教你怎么拍出 Ins 照的文章；这些都在破坏我们的旅游。随着 Ins 效应在 2019 年持续不衰，各个旅游目的地也开始想办法反击了——他们要想办法挡住那些成群结队挥舞自拍杆的游客。

这 5 个景点正在对抗 Ins 效应：

天空之岛，苏格兰

Ins 上的旅游网红们特别喜欢去拍天空之岛上的仙子湖、埃尔戈尔的落日以及老人岩。然而这座小岛的基础设施承载不了这么多车流，这就导致了人潮拥挤、交通堵塞以及游客素质低下等问题。在 2017 年，内希布里丁岛的警察就警告人们说：如果没有订到住宿，就不要来。

杜布罗夫尼克，克罗地亚

由于《权力的游戏》，这座城市的旧城已经挤满了游客，全都在"君临城"自拍。为了对抗人潮，这座城市现在已经限制了停靠邮轮和造访游客的数量。在 2017 年，杜布罗夫尼克把每日的游客数限制在了 8000 人，而且还有摄像头监控；而 2019 年即将出台的新规可能会把这个限额减半。

斯凯利哥·迈克尔岛，爱尔兰

《星球大战》中天行者卢克的居所：这个"原力觉醒"的拍摄地点已经变成越来越流行的旅游目的地了，2017 年几乎有 17000 人来这儿。现在，联合国教科文组织的世界遗产网站只允许每天 180 名游客来这，其原因是为了让大自然不受游客的干扰。

马略卡岛，西班牙

旅游过剩曾在这个巴利亚群岛的一员上引发过所谓的"夏日行动"，参与行动的人对酒店进行了打砸抢，还在机场示威，并且举着"旅游正在杀死这座城市"的标语。据《电讯报》报道，政府的应对方法是把游客税翻倍了，每人每天需要交 4 欧元，差不多 4.64 美元。

根据《CN旅游》报道，他们还打击了诸如Airbnb一类的短租服务，"几乎禁止一切租赁，除了那些不在机场附近也不在公地之内的偏远住房。"

马丘比丘，秘鲁

根据《CN旅游》报道，秘鲁政府在2015年宣布了一个5年4370万美元计划来保护这处遗迹。在2017年，他们开始限制游客的入场时间，每天只有两个区间；同时他们还要求游客必须由经过认证的导游陪同，而且游客在遗迹中的行程被限制在了特定的路线上。每天只供应5000张门票，这已经高于联合国教科文组织建议数量的两倍了。今年，他们的旅游管制进一步走严了，时间限制是4小时，而且不得重复入园。

Part V Discussion

Work in pairs. Role-play a conversation between an after-sales clerk and an important customer. The conversation should involve the following aspects.

The customer has been doing business with the company for over ten years.
The Spring Festival is coming.
The after-sales clerk visits the customer.
The after-sales clerk wants to thank the customer for his cooperation with the company.

Part VI Writing

Task: Your restaurant has received a letter of complaint about his bad experience in the restaurant. Write an adjustment letter for it.

Sample

Dear Mr. Taylor,

Thank you for your letter of March 12.

We are sorry that the sweater washed by our laundry department was stretched out. It might have been stretched out during washing. And we also apologize for the rude attitude of the receptionist, who will be published according to our hotel's service policy.

We will make up for the incident as soon as possible. Our after-sales clerk will contact you to make sure the way of compensation.

Please accept our apology for the inconvenience it has caused.

Yours sincerely,
Rose Tan
Customer Service Manager

参考文献

[1] 徐小贞. 新职业英语[M]. 北京：外语教学与研究出版社，2018.
[2] 陈的非，刘建金. 旅游英语[M]. 北京：中国轻工业出版社，2012.
[3] 段开成，黄宝琴. 旅游英语（初级）[M]. 天津：南开大学出版社，1999.
[4] 本书编写组. 酒店服务英语[M]. 北京：中国旅游出版社，2010.
[5] 钱嘉颖，吴云. 酒店英语口译[M]. 上海：上海交通大学出版社，2016.
[6] 谢大光. 百年外国散文精华[M]. 杭州：浙江文艺出版社，2007.
[7] The gripes of broth[N]. Economist, 2019, 4(3).